Creating a New Profession

The Beginnings of Social Work Education in the United States

Leslie Leighninger

Council on Social Work Education
Alexandria, VA

Copyright © 2000 by the Council on Social Work Education, Inc.

All rights reserved. No part of this book may be reproduced or transmitted in any manner whatsoever without the prior written permission of the publisher, Council on Social Work Education, Inc., 1725 Duke Street, Suite 500, Alexandria, VA 22314-3457.

Library of Congress Cataloging-in-Publication Data

Leighninger, Leslie.
Creating a new profession: the beginnings of social work education in the United States / Leslie Leighninger.
    p. cm.
Includes bibliographical references.
ISBN 0-87293-076-9
    1. Social work education—United States—History. I. Title.
HV11.7.L45 2000
361.3'2'071073—dc21   00-023828
                                                                                                                   CIP

Manufactured in the United States of America.

Contents

Preface v

1. **A Call for Action** 1

    Anna L. Dawes, "The Need of Training Schools
    for a New Profession" 3

    Mary Richmond, "The Need of a Training School
    in Applied Philanthropy" 7

2. **The First Training Schools in Social Work** 11

    Jeffrey R. Brackett, "Present Opportunities for
    Training in Charitable Work" 13

3. **Parallel Paths** 19

    George E. Haynes, "Cooperation with Colleges
    in Securing and Training Negro Social Workers
    for Urban Centers" 22

    Forrester B. Washington, "The Need and
    Education of Negro Social Workers" 27

4. **The Relationship between Social Work Training
    and the Development of a Profession** 37

    Abraham Flexner, "Is Social Work a Profession?" 39

    Edward T. Devine, "A Profession in the Making" 48

5. **The Shape of the Emerging Professional Education
    for Social Work** 51

    Edith Abbott, "Education for Social Work" 55

    Zilpha Smith, "Field Work" 62

    Mary Richmond, from *Social Diagnosis* 66

References 85

Preface

In 1910, a new field called "social work" boasted five professional training schools in the United States. Now, 90 years later, that number has increased more than a hundredfold, to 126 accredited graduate schools of social work and 410 accredited undergraduate programs. All but three states have graduate social work education; every state offers social work education at the baccalaureate level (Lennon, 1999). In 1998, these programs granted over 13,500 MSW degrees and about 11,400 BSW degrees.

The pioneers in professional social work education—people like Mary Richmond, Jeffrey Brackett, Edward Devine, George Haynes, and Edith Abbott—would be astounded at the number, quality, and broad geographical distribution of social work schools and programs. Yet if the pioneers could visit this "new world," they would also note much that is familiar, including the continued emphasis on "scientific knowledge" and research, the stress placed on field work, the attempt to keep up with new techniques and technology, the significance of race and gender, the search for balance between client-centered and societal perspectives, and the constant pull in classroom teaching between the "theoretical" and the "practical." Then and now, social work schools and programs have constituted a central arena for making sense of what Linda Shoemaker (1998) calls the "multiple roots and competing visions of social work" (183).

To understand the shape of today's social work education, it is helpful to return to the words of the first social work professional leaders and educators. Their names and activities are chronicled, at least briefly, in introductory social work texts. Yet we rarely get the full flavor of their ideas, aspirations, and enthusiasm for the education of an emerging profession. This monograph, coming at the beginning of a new century for social work, aims to impart an understanding of where we started, primarily through the words of social work's pioneers. In the chapters that follow, the founders of social work education speak for themselves; excerpted from speeches and writings, their vision for educating social workers comes alive.

1. A Call for Action

> What is needed, it seems to me, is some course of study where an intelligent young person can...be taught the alphabet of charitable science.
>
> Anna Dawes

A major thread in the development of social work education as a profession in the United States was the rise of the Charity Organization Society movement in the late 1800s. Criticizing the work of existing philanthropic groups as superficial almsgiving with little organized investigation of recipients, the new charity organization societies sought to build a more ordered and scientific approach to working with the poor. Particularly in the early years of the movement, the societies' work was based on the belief that dependency was largely a matter of individual responsibility rather than social forces. Based on this interpretation of the causes of poverty, the societies assigned volunteer "friendly visitors" to needy families. These visitors were to correct the character flaws of the poor and to inspire them to strive for independence (Lubove, 1969; Trattner, 1999).

The work of the friendly visitors called for more than good intentions. The new scientific charity required special knowledge, skills, and techniques. At first, charity organizations tried to impart these through apprenticeship and other training arrangements. In some organizations, more experienced staff trained new workers; in others, new recruits attended special classes to learn basic procedures. Yet it soon became clear that such on-the-job, rule-of-thumb training could not give people the broad principles and theory necessary for a consistent and effective practice of charitable work. In addition, as those engaged in social work began to think of its potential as a new profession, the idea of formal education in applied philanthropy became more and more appealing.

The charity organization movement leader Mary Richmond is usually credited with the definitive call for establishment of formal training in social work. Yet Richmond's speech at the 1897 meeting of the National Conference of Charities and Correction was preceded by a paper delivered by Anna L. Dawes at the International Congress of

Charities and Correction at the Chicago World's Fair in 1893. Dawes was a community leader involved in charity work in Springfield, Massachusetts; the main impetus for her call for training was frustration over the difficulty of finding a knowledgeable director of charities in this small New England city.

Despite Dawes' hesitancy at introducing the topic to an international audience, it is likely that her message struck a cord not only with American participants at the charities meeting, but also with their European counterparts. As Katherine A. Kendall notes in *Social Work Education: Its Origins in Europe*, published in conjunction with this volume, by 1899 a school of social work would be established in Amsterdam, to be followed shortly by schools in England and Germany.

Although Dawes delivered her paper when social work was just beginning, several points should be familiar to today's social worker. She notes the eager practitioner with "his head full of science" (or theory), who knows little about applying his knowledge. She also draws attention to the low level of salaries in charity work. In addition, she acknowledges the importance of gender issues. Although Dawes follows the accepted practice of using the masculine pronoun to indicate both men and women, in the fuller version of her speech she comments that the masculine pronoun "becomes specific" when one talks about the charity director who must "present his cause at public meetings." Although she admits to some ambivalence about the situation, she concludes that:

> Except in special cases a man has more influence and carries more weight with the business men of the town in presenting matters of charity and public welfare than a woman. I do not discuss the reasons for this, nor its justice; I simply state it as a fact, and I think it cannot be disputed. (Dawes, p. 15)

This sense of "having to face reality" about society's greater readiness to give credence to men's ideas over women's will haunt many women social work leaders and educators for years to come.

Anna L. Dawes
The Need of Training Schools for a New Profession*

It is hardly fitting that the time of an International Congress like this should be occupied with the details of charity organization, details which must necessarily be to some extent local in their character. It is obvious that the problems of administration which beset us in America can hardly be the problems which beset English philanthropists, much less those of Germany or Italy. Indeed, to go farther than this, it is a question whether the problems that are current in Massachusetts are in any degree the problems of Colorado or California, or even, it may be, of Illinois. But a certain difficulty which we are experiencing every day in New England seems to me to be a difficulty inseparable from the growth and extension of the methods of scientific charity, and so everywhere existent. And therefore, although it is perhaps a minor question in the survey of the whole field, I have ventured to ask you to consider it for a very brief time, that we may get the benefit of your wisdom upon it, and that, if you will, the great influence of this body may be given in favor of some solution of the problem. For it is not my intention to suggest a solution at this time, but simply to bring before you the need, the difficulty of meeting it, and the nature of the remedy that others wiser than I may discover how the end shall be accomplished....

As the plan of charity organization extends beyond the large cities into the smaller cities and towns...we are met with the difficulty of procuring suitable men or women as secretaries or superintendents of the work. This amounts to an impossibility. It is unnecessary to say to anyone of experience in these matters, that practically the whole success of the undertaking depends upon the officer who administers its affairs, whether known as superintendent or secretary, and whether man or woman....The services of such a superintendent as I have outlined, varied and difficult as they are, must be secured for a salary ranging from seven hundred to one thousand dollars a year....I do not discuss the justice of this situation, I simply state a fact....

The position [of secretary or superintendent] is open, therefore, to two classes of persons—that large class of able and efficient young men

---

* From A. G. Warner (Ed.), *Sociology in Institutions of Learning*, pp. 14–20. Baltimore, MD: Johns Hopkins Press, 1894.

and women who, without other than a public school education, are satisfied, at least temporarily, with such a salary as I have named; and that other class who from a missionary impulse put better education and larger capacity at the service of the public, for only such remuneration as will furnish them a not too abundant livelihood. This class is happily growing more and more numerous every day as the zeal for humanity and the better understanding of religion increases among us. The claims of the poor in our cities and towns are being felt, and they are making a loud call to our generous minded young men and women....

Now whether you look in the ranks of the wage-earner or the philanthropist, it is today impossible to get a suitable superintendent of charities for a city of fifteen or twenty thousand inhabitants (or even a larger city), because no one knows anything about how to carry on the work. The wage-earner knows absolutely nothing of scientific charity. He has never heard of "friendly visitors"; he knows nothing of the merits or demerits of outdoor relief; boys' clubs have no attractions for him, and he fails lamentably in the effort to manage them; prison reform is so far an unknown language that he has no ideas as to discharged prisoners or probationers; and night lodging houses and woodyards are equally beyond his ken. Charity is so little of a science to him that he can neither understand the idea himself, nor force it into the mind of an unwilling public. On the other hand, the young man of missionary impulses has his head full of the science, but his opportunities for the practice of the art have been too meagre for valuable results. He has no experience on which to draw for the detection of fraud, he has no knowledge of the practical difficulties of administration which will confront him in a community unsympathetic, and unwilling to contribute for the support of a charity which has no visible results, and skeptical of the need of anything beyond the usual public relief....

I am convinced that it is not so much lack of willing individuals as entire lack of opportunity for training that is the real trouble....What is needed, it seems to me, is some course of study where an intelligent young person can add to an ordinary education such branches as may be necessary for this purpose, with a general view of those special studies in political and social science which are most closely connected with the problem of poverty; and where both he and his associate, already learned in the study of books, can be taught what is now the alphabet of charitable science—some knowledge of its underlying ideas, its tried and trusted methods, and some acquaintance with the various devices employed for the upbuilding of the needy, so that no philanthropic undertaking, from a model tenement-house to a kindergarten to a sand heap, will be altogether strange to his mind. Some more immediately practical experience of the work likely to be required should also be given, some laboratory practice in the science of charity, if we may so speak. And this course should be made under such auspices and should cover so brief a period, should be so superficial if you choose to say so, that it need not be unduly expensive. For the *sine qua non* of this profession is the possibility of procuring trained workers for a moderate salary. The day must come soon when this shall be possible, or the whole scheme will fall to the ground so far as any localities except the large cities are concerned.

The only purpose of these few words is to bring before this body the need of such workers, the possible supply, and the entire lack of any opportunity for learning the science and the art of charity. It seems to me that the time has come when either through a course in some established institution, or in an institution by itself, or by the old-fashioned method never yet improved upon for actual development—the method of experimental training as the personal assistant of some skilled worker—it ought to be possible for those who would take up this work to find some place for studying it as a profession. And it is because I have felt that this must be a problem common to all countries, and urgent in all localities, that I have ventured to bring it before this body to-day and to ask for your views upon it.

Dawes thus laid out a tentative proposal for a brief and practical course of study to meet the immediate staffing needs of charitable agencies. It fell to Mary Richmond to produce a more substantive plan for educating charity workers. Unlike most charity organization leaders, Richmond did not come from a well-to-do family, and while she graduated from a girl's school highly respected for its academic rigor, she did not attend college. After a series of clerical and bookkeeping jobs, she took a position as assistant treasurer of the Baltimore Charity Organization Society. Here she met prominent woman reformers who served as mentors and friends. With their support, Richmond became the director of the Baltimore COS in 1891, a post formerly held by men with graduate training. She quickly rose to prominence in the charity movement (Pittman-Munke, 1986; Pumphrey, 1986).

Like Dawes, Richmond realized the pressing need for education in charitable work, but she had a broader perspective regarding the potential of what she called "applied philanthropy." She communicated her ideas at the annual meeting of the National Conference of Charities and Correction, a gathering of officials of state charitable institutions, settlement workers, and charity workers. The meeting served as an important forum for the discussion of new ideas and practices in charitable work and social reform.

Richmond's concern was that the field of philanthropy had already become highly specialized. She felt its true strength lay in the discovery of a common ground among people involved in the different types of charitable endeavor. Such a common ground, established by a training school, would be an important step toward establishing social work as a profession. Richmond's comments on specialization in charity work, the need for a common base of knowledge, and the relationship between education and practice bear a similarity to discussions about social work education today. In addition, her interest in social work's professional development anticipates the field's perennial concern over its status as a profession. Finally, you will note that Richmond uses analogies to the medical profession which were to become more and more common as social workers assessed their achievement of that status.

Mary E. Richmond

Secretary, Charity Organization Society, Baltimore, MD

The Need of a Training School in Applied Philanthropy*

It is just twenty years since certain new ideas about the administration of charities came to have currency among us in the United States, and led to the founding of voluntary associations known as charity organization societies. The question now is how to get educated young men and women to make a life vocation of charity organization work. We must educate them. Through these twenty years our charity organization societies have stood for trained service in charity. We are thoroughly committed to that, in theory at least. But it is not enough to create a demand for trained service. Having created the demand (and I think we may claim that our share in its creation has been considerable), we should strive to supply it.

Moreover, we owe it to those who shall come after us that they shall be spared the groping and blundering by which we have acquired our own stock of experience. In these days of specialization, when we train our cooks, our apothecaries, our engineers, our librarians, our nurses,—when, in fact, there is a training school for almost every form of skilled service,—we have yet to establish our first training school for charity workers, or, as I prefer to call it, "Training School in Applied Philanthropy."

It is only gradually that the need of such a school has made itself apparent; but I was not surprised, upon writing a few months ago to a number of workers, engaged in different branches of charity work in different sections of the country, to find that the idea had occurred to several of them. We have known for a long while that we wanted young people of high character and unusual attainments to devote themselves to a cause which has seemed to us of the first importance; but we are just beginning to understand that these young people have a right to demand something of us in return. Surely, they have a right to demand from the profession of applied philanthropy (we really have not even a name for it) that which they have a right to demand from any other

---

* From I. C. Barrows (Ed.), *Proceedings of the National Conference of Charities and Correction*, pp. 181–187. Boston: George H. Ellis, 1898.

profession,—further opportunities for education and development, and incidentally, the opportunity to earn a living.

Now the opportunities for education and development must always be extremely limited in any calling which has not established a professional standard, a certain fairly definite outline of what the practitioner in that field is expected to know and to be. We are all agreed, I think, that such a standard is desirable. But the matter about which we are likely to differ is this: Some of us will think that a training school is impracticable until we have acquired a professional standard, and others will think that we can never acquire a professional standard until we have the school. This latter is my own view, though I would avoid, if possible, the clamorous solicitude about it of a hen who has only one chick. It may be that we are not quite ready for the school, that such a plan is premature. If so, I urge that we should begin to move without delay in the direction, at least, of some definite system of training.

Let me borrow, as we continually are tempted to borrow in our charity work, a few illustrations from the medical profession. I have been reminded that the analogy between the charitable and the medical professions is not a true one, that the science of medicine is a far more highly organized body of knowledge. For that very reason we so often turn to the physicians: they are what we merely hope to be. We ourselves may be said to have advanced no further than that rudimentary stage of charitable progress where our barbers let blood and pull teeth....We know that even in the medical profession almost every crude form of earlier practice still survives; but these survivals are weighed and found wanting by a definite professional standard, and such a standard is sadly needed in our charity, to discredit unintelligent work. I am little versed in medical history; but is it not probable that the profession of medicine owes a large part of its inheritance of knowledge and principles to its schools, which have established the tradition that the members of a liberal profession should be not only practitioners, but teachers?

An experienced worker has written to me that a difficulty in the way of a school of applied philanthropy on a sufficiently broad and inclusive basis would be the fact that our charity work has become so highly specialized. This is true, but our specialization is often essentially false. It is still as erratic as the specialization of the barber who pulls teeth. In the division of modern medicine into many special departments we find few such anomalies. We find, moreover, a broad field of knowledge which is common ground....What an incalculable gain to humanity when those who are doctoring social diseases in many departments of charitable work shall [also] have found a common ground of agreement, and be forced to recognize certain established principles as underlying all effective service! Not immediately, of course, but slowly and steadily, such a common ground could be established, I believe, by a training school for our professional workers.

This question presents itself in different ways, according as one looks at it with reference to the needs of small or large towns, of public or private charities, or institutions or societies. Miss Anna L. Dawes who was the first one to suggest the need of a training school for our new profession, conceived the idea after unavailing efforts to find a suitable superintendent for the charitable society of a small city....

Working, as I do, in the charity organization society of a large city, the matter has presented itself to me in a somewhat different way. Like some other charity organization societies, we give our agents a preliminary training in charitable theory and practice; but this training specializes too soon, and our leaders have felt the need of a more intimate and sympathetic acquaintance on the part of our agents with child-saving work, almshouse work, reformatory work, care of defectives, and all the other branches of work represented at this Conference. We feel, of course, that every form of charity could be improved by a better knowledge of charity organization principles; but it seems to us of the first importance, also, that our agents should have a better all-round knowledge of other forms of charity. The school that is to be most helpful to our charity organization agents, therefore, must be established on a broad basis, and be prepared to train relief agents, child-saving agents, institution officials, and other charitable specialists. An important part of their training would be in that shoulder-to-shoulder contact which makes cooperation natural and inevitable.

I recognize that all this is very vague. Let me venture a step further. Before anything is settled about our training school in applied philanthropy save the bare fact that such a school is needed we should search the country for the right man to organize it. We need a university-trained man who is now engaged in charitable work, and who has had wide, practical experience in it ....[To] succeed, he must believe that a training school for charity workers is necessary and practicable, and he must be guaranteed time, money, and entire freedom of action, together with the hearty support of our leading charitable specialists.

You will observe that, having found one man, it will become immediately necessary to find another, to furnish the money for this experiment. And this, to some, is like to be the rock on which our new craft might go to pieces. But consider the things that people do spend money for. I remember to have heard of the experiments of a psychologist for which an American millionaire has been furnishing large sums of money. By some very complicated machinery the experimenter hopes to determine the colors of our emotional states. Now, if such fanciful science as that can find a patron, why should our school go a-begging if we can once heartily agree that it is practical?

Given the money and the head master, I can imagine that the latter's first care would be to make a detailed inquiry into the paid service demanded by our charities. His next would be to determine the school's location and affiliations. Probably he would choose a large city,—the larger the better; and it may be that he would seek connection with some institution of learning, though it should never be forgotten that emphasis is to be put on practical work rather than on academic requirements. Vital connection, therefore, would of necessity be made with the public and private charities of the city. Here students could observe the actual work of charity, and take part in it under the daily supervision of their instructors. Theory and practice would go hand and hand, and our best specialists would be engaged to deliver courses of lectures during the less busy months of the year. A two years' course would probably begin with general principles, and would specialize later, so that all regular students would take some of the courses together. Nor would the needs of special students, such as those who could spare only a few months, be overlooked; and probably volunteers who are interested in some particular charity would be glad to avail themselves of the school's opportunities.

I offer this plan in all its crudity, without attempting any elaboration, because I feel that it needs, and I trust will receive, the frankest criticism. There is often only a little difference between knowing and not knowing. I would not, therefore, exaggerate the importance of merely technical training....[More] important than any training in detail is the opportunity which a good school would offer for the development of higher ideals of charitable service. "Ideals are catching," some one has said. How important, then, to send our young people, our future workers, where ideals can be "caught"! A friend of mine is in the habit of saying, in praise of a college, that its graduates are never ashamed to acknowledge their ignorance, that the school has given all its pupils a certain candid habit of thought. To give our professional charity workers better habits of thought and higher ideals, this should be the chief aim of our School of Applied Philanthropy. I need not say how slowly a good school grows, or how slowly it makes its influence felt. But, if these twenty years have taught us anything, they have taught us that plans which are to find their full realization the year after next are not worth initiating. The chief and perhaps the only claim which this rough sketch of a plan can have to consideration is to be found in the willingness of its advocate to leave much to the future.

2. The First Training Schools in Social Work

> The spontaneity of nature's provision for the needs of life characterizes and accounts for the rise of the specialized educational efforts to train for philanthropic and social service....On both its practical and academic side this development has been wholly natural, if not inevitable, at just this stage of the evolution of philanthropy.
>
> Graham Taylor

Most social workers have only a general picture of the intitial development of social work education: Mary Richmond gave a speech in 1897, and the New York Summer School in Philanthropic Work—the "first school of social work"—is established in the following year. The real picture is more complicated, with a variety of kinds of training emerging for charity work and broader types of social work from the mid-1890s on. As Richmond noted in her talk at the National Conference, individual charity organizations had already begun to develop what we would now call "in-service training sessions" for their staff. The practice of apprenticeship, where a new worker was guided by an experienced one, was common. Some charity organizations were experimenting with short term "study classes," in which charity workers and other interested individuals could read and discuss relevant books and conference papers (Brackett, 1903). Taking a broader and more academic approach, universities had begun to offer courses in economics and sociology that included discussion of social issues and social reform. Leaders in the settlement house movement shared this interest in education for work that went beyond the charity approach to a focus on social change. In 1895, Graham Taylor, who founded the settlement Chicago Commons, launched a series of lectures housed at the Commons. Taylor described the series as a "periodical conference of Settlement workers, ministers and others interested in social questions and social work" (as cited in Coohey, 1999, p. 418).

People like Dawes, Richmond, and Jeffrey Brackett regarded all these forms of education as insufficient for the broad yet practice-focused preparation of the charity worker. The head of the Department of Charities and Corrections in Baltimore, Brackett had established a reputation for his important contributions to charity organization and public welfare in that city. Like Richmond, he believed that the future of professional social work lay in the strength of its educational programs (Lubove, 1969, p. 141). In the following excerpt, Brackett heralds the formation of the New York Summer School as an important first step in developing "real training" in charitable work. Note his distinction between that training and the "instruction" offered in more traditional academic settings.

ഈഃ

Jeffrey R. Brackett

President of Department of Charities and Corrections, Baltimore, MD

Present Opportunities for Training in Charitable Work*

The president of Harvard University, that great educator and great man, has said, "As a people, we do not apply to mental activities the principal for the division of labor, and we have but a halting faith in special training for high professional employments." This National Conference has proclaimed year by year the conviction that work in charity and correction which is worthy of the name of charity, which aims at a cure, reformation, prevention, requires mental activity, and should be classed as a high calling. What opportunities are there now in this country for training in charitable work? Are we using our opportunities as we should?

Let us distinguish first between training and instruction. Of late there has been a noteworthy increase in the number of universities, colleges, and theological schools which offer courses more or less on public aid, charity, and correction. That academic work, well done, is of great value; but, speaking generally, because briefly, it is essentially instruction, the imparting of information,—it is not essentially training. Academic work, after all, is chiefly to lead the mind to think accurately, to weigh justly causes and results in any field of knowledge. Its chief contribution today to the cause of charity is in doing that, and in so arousing the interest of students, through special instruction, that, when they go out into various duties here and there, they will promote progressive charitable work.

Those who take up charitable work as a calling of chief interest, whether paid or as volunteers, whether or not they have been to college, need to get as quickly and as well as they can, with as little waste to themselves and others, the element which enters with instruction into education,—experience. If possible, they should be trained by persons of experience.

We are familiar with training schools in many fields of activity, as in medicine, school-teaching, church work. The Young Men's Christian

---

* From I. C. Barrows (Ed.), *Proceedings of the National Conference of Charities and Correction*, pp. 289–293. Boston: George H. Ellis, 1901.

Associations can get secretaries from their training school, with its three-year course. Librarians are now trained in special schools.

The Boston Associated Charities began a few years ago—and Baltimore has since followed—the rule of a certain period of instruction and training by the general secretary for applicants for the positions of district agents. The agreement is that they drop out after a reasonable amount of training, if they prove to be lacking in characteristics essential to their own success and the welfare of the society and the needy. The more we can get the right men and women at the heads of our institutions and agencies, the more will these become training schools, as the master used to train his apprentice and the doctor his student.

Despite the earnest pleas of Miss Dawes, Miss Richmond, and others at several of our Conferences since 1892, there is as yet no training school for charity workers to which any properly qualified person may readily turn for a sufficiently long term of instruction combined with real training. But the "class in philanthropic work" conducted by the Charity Organization Society of the city of New York in the summer of 1898, and repeated the two summers following, has become the Summer School in Philanthropic Work under a special committee of the society, with representatives from other societies, and begins its fourth session in June next.

The details of this school are to be found in the reports of the New York society and the *Charities Review*. I call to your attention, however, the following facts. For six weeks of each of the past three summers, from twenty to thirty men and women have attended lectures, taken part in discussions, made special inquiries, visited institutions and agencies, worked with experienced workers in charity and correction. Last year the twenty-four students registered for the full course, and the six present for portions of it, included graduates from fifteen universities and colleges and workers of some experience from thirteen charitable organizations. They came from eleven states. Three weeks were given to the subject of the care of destitute, neglected, and delinquent children; another week to neighborhood improvements; and another week was divided between medical charities and institutional care of adults. The method of the school is practical. The speakers are leaders in their lines of work; and some of them, spending several days with the members of the class, add the personal acquaintance and opportunities for informal talks.

The requirements for admission include a degree from a college or a year of actual service done in philanthropic work. The aim is to get those persons who have given reasonable promise of intelligent, useful activity.

The committee in charge, knowing that no class lasting for a few weeks, or even for a few months, can give a real training, are asking for money to establish several fellowships, which will allow some members of the school to make special inquiries and to do work under persons of experience for periods of a year at least. The school now gives a bird's-eye view of the wide field of opportunities, with points of special interest carefully pointed out by those who know them well....

All such educational work can be made more effective now because we have in this National Conference and in local conferences, in the growing current literature of charity, notably *Charities,* a means of keeping somewhat in touch with other workers and thinkers. *Charities* should be to us what the best medical journal is to the physician....

The aim of the members of this Conference is to lessen pauperism and crime, suffering and evil. Many influences will help us. But these meetings teach one great lesson: we must increase in more and more communities more wide-spread and earnest conviction that the person who can best work out the needed methods for any given time and place are those—paid officials or volunteers—who can add to natural good parts a high purpose, a reasonable knowledge of the experience of others' work, and to that a reasonable knowledge of the needs and possibilities of those for whom they care.

In conclusion, let us acknowledge the debt we all owe to the New York Charity Organization Society and the Boston Associated Charities,—to the former for founding and fostering the *Charities Review* and the Summer School in Philanthropic Work, to the latter for keeping before us the great truth that most effective work for the needy is based on a knowledge by personal experience of their needs and possibilities. These societies have shown us the beginning of the way,—a long and steep but lofty reaching way.

Calls for training schools for a new profession were at last answered. Three years after Brackett's 1901 address, the New York Summer School became a full-time, eight-month program of study under the new name of the New York School of Philanthropy. It was still a free-standing school, sponsored by the New York Charity Organization Society, and not affiliated with a university. The school's handbook of 1904 noted that enrollment was open to those "engaged in some form of philanthropic activity as a profession," as well as college graduates, advanced students in medicine, nursing, and sociology, and volunteers in philanthropic organizations (Coohey, 1999, p. 420). In 1905, the New York School was established on a more permanent basis through an endowment from philanthropist John S. Kennedy, who stipulated that the school develop an affiliation with Columbia University. This was to be carried out through the participation of "the presidents of the four leading charitable societies of the City and the president of Columbia University" as ex-officio members of the school's guiding committee. The affiliation with Columbia remained a loose one, however. Through its strong ties with the Charity Organization Society, the New York School retained its status as an independent school of social work for over 50 years (Dore, 1999; Taylor, 1905, pp. 440–441).

Other cities were also establishing professional training schools in the same general time period. It is in fact difficult to establish which was the first training school for the new profession, since the shape and evolution of these institutions differed greatly. Some began as summer schools, some as full-time programs; some focused on the broader field of social issues and social reform, while others stressed education for charity workers. Some offered admission only to those with degrees (and could therefore be called "graduate schools"), while others, such as the New York School, did not limit admission to college graduates (Coohey, 1999). What is more significant than who came first is the several varieties in this experiment in educating people for the new career of social work, and the influences the various schools had on the developing profession.

The Boston School for Social Workers, which Brackett himself helped establish in 1904, bore some similarity to the New York School. It too was supported by a charity organization, the Boston Associated Charities, and focused on preparation for charity work. But its university affiliation, which was a dual connection with both Harvard and Simmons College, was more formal. Courses in the school constituted the last year of a four-year program at Simmons, and resulted in a B.A. (in a sense an earlier type of BSW education). The school's program was also part of a double course in the Department of Social Ethics at Harvard (Brackett, 1906).

In Philadelphia, The University of Pennsylvania School of Social Work began as a short course within the University in 1908. Interest in professional education had been stimulated by leaders in the field of child welfare. St. Louis saw the establishment of a School of Philanthropy in 1907, affiliated first with the University of Missouri, then with Washington University, and then back again, after a year of independence, with the University of Missouri. Graham Taylor's lecture series in Chicago became an Institute of Social Science and Arts in 1904, with courses offered through the University of Chicago's extension program. The school lost its connection with the University of Chicago two years later (Brackett, 1906; Lubove, 1969). In 1908, after receiving foundation funding, the program re-emerged as the freestanding Chicago School of Civics and Philanthropy.

I give this detail in part to suggest the fluidity of sponsorship and affiliation in those early days, as well as what was often an ambivalence about the appropriateness of a formal university setting for social work training. As one social work educator noted in 1905

> If perchance a training school for philanthropic workers is supported by a University, it seems to me that there is danger, even if its teaching force is chosen from practical workers, that its courses will become either very general and...academic, or else dogmatic; and in order to [help unfortunates] without having the new worker gain his experience at their expense, we must have more than generalities; and there is no room at all for dogmatism. (P. Ayres, as cited in Taylor, 1905, p. 439)

On the other hand, as Taylor commented:

> So long as there is a actually joint control of these schools [by] practical and academic experts...the danger of becoming doctrinaire is far less than the manifest gain both to the university and to all lines of practical work in the alliance of the academic spirit and scientific method with the laboratory practice and the human touch. (p. 441)

Much of the discussion regarding sponsorship, goals, and other issues in the emerging professional education took place at meetings of the Committee on Training of Social Workers, which was established within the National Conference of Charities and Correction in 1905. Graham Taylor was the group's first chair. The committee included major figures in the charity movement, such as Richmond and Brackett, along with well known sociologists and economists, such as Richard T. Ely of the University of Wisconsin and Charles Henderson of the University of Chicago. Although it had no responsibility for setting educational standards or approving curriculum, the group could be seen as a rudimentary form of educational association, paving the way for the establishment of the American Association of Schools of Social Work, with 17 charter schools, in 1919.

3. Parallel Paths

> It is the object of the Atlanta School of Social Service to afford an opportunity for training in the principles and technique of social work to colored young men and women. Trained Negro leadership in solving the social problems of the South is essential.
>
> Announcement, Atlanta School of Social Service at Morehouse College, 1920.

Although in the early years the field of social work was predominately white and Protestant, it also included Jewish, Catholic, and African-American practitioners. Jewish and Catholic groups often developed their own social agencies and schools. Jewish social workers operated family agencies and established a national conference of Jewish social work. Catholic social work was organized in central diocesan agencies, generally called Catholic Charities. Leaders in both movements saw the need for specialized training, and had by the 1920s established such schools such as the Training School for Jewish Social Work and Fordham University in New York City, and the National Catholic Social Service School (later to become Catholic University) in Washington, D.C. All three were members of the American Association of Schools of Social Work (Karpf, 1925; Leighninger, 1987; Popple & Leighninger, 1999).

To some degree, at least, Catholic and Jewish social workers chose to maintain a separate identity within social work. African Americans faced a much more serious situation of exclusion. Several prominent African-American social workers did play influential roles in forums like the National Conference of Social Work (as the National Conference of Charities and Correction was renamed in 1917). Yet by and large the black social work community experienced little acceptance in the field. African Americans were rarely found on the staffs of large city charity organization societies or family agencies. Because of segregation laws and customs, African Americans were generally unable to enroll in white graduate schools or to do their internships in white social work organizations. These agencies were often segregated, working with African-American clients in separate facilities, if at all (Johnson, 1978). The little training that existed consisted of short-term courses, or training institutes, sponsored by social welfare agencies, sometimes with the help of universities.

Exclusion from the white social welfare system had early on led African Americans to develop their own responses to the needs of their communities. Often through the work of African American women's clubs and churches, blacks developed their own network of charitable organizations and established settlement houses, children's nurseries, and homes for the aged. (Carlton-LaNey, 1994; Scott, 1993). This "separate path" of African American social welfare led to the same call for professional training as in white social work circles. The following two selections give examples of responses to that call.

The author of the first selection, George Haynes, served as the first director of the National Urban League, which he helped found in 1910. Haynes was born in a small Arkansas community, where his mother worked as a domestic servant and his father as an occasional laborer. Haynes' mother instilled in him strong religious and moral ideas and a belief in the importance of education. A visit to the Chicago World's Fair exposed Hayes to the philosophical and political ferment among urban African-American communities and helped convince him that the problems of blacks in America would be solved through interracial cooperation in creating equity and justice. Improved education for African Americans would help in achieving such equity (Popple & Leighninger, 1999).

After graduating from Yale University, Haynes worked as a Secretary of the Colored Men's Department of the international YMCA. This experience led him to enroll in the New York School of Philanthropy and to become its first black graduate in 1910. It was his connection with the New York School, which did not discriminate against black applicants, that led to Haynes' development of the cooperative social work training program between the school and Fisk University.

Forrester B. Washington was another important pioneer in African American social work education. Washington was born in Salem, Massachusetts. Like Haynes, he was well-educated, having earned a bachelor's degree from Tufts College in 1909 and a master's degree from Columbia University eight years later. Also like Haynes, Washington worked in leadership positions in the Urban League. Washington served as dean of the Atlanta University School of Social Work from 1927 to 1954. The school had begun within Morehouse College in 1919, and was incorporated and chartered under its first director, sociologist E. Franklin Frazier, in 1924 (Ross, 1978; Peebles-Wilkins, 1995a, 1995b).

In their writings, both men note the special problems of the African American population in the United States and the ways in which social work could respond to these. Washington speaks specifically to the issue of whether whites can work effectively with African-American clients, and concludes that only black social workers can truly understand the black situation. The question of whether "like" social workers should work with "like" clients is still debated today.

George E. Haynes
Professor, Fisk University

Cooperation with Colleges in Securing and Training Negro Social Workers for Urban Centers[*]

While my paper discusses a plan for uniting the Negro college, the professional school and social work among Negroes in urban centers, it has a grain of suggestion which may be generally applied in securing and training white students for social work.

It is only necessary to remind you of the fact that there is an increasing concentration of Negroes in urban centers, and a pressing problem for the Negro is to learn to live in town.

This urban situation, like many other human problems, is fundamentally one of efficient men and women who are thoroughly devoted to the special service in which they are engaged. The condition among Negroes in cities can best be improved by those of their own group whose latent capacity has had superior training directed toward social service.

The youth in Negro colleges furnish the key to the situation, for those less thoroughly trained will not be able to grapple successfully with such serious conditions. Several schools of Philanthropy are open to Negro students, but these institutions are out of the reach of nearly all of them. Several Negro colleges have offered courses in Economics and Sociology, but in nearly every case they have been scarcely more than class room discussions, often remotely relating to conditions among Negroes. So it is safe to say that, until we started last year, there had been no definite training for social work offered anywhere for Negro students and no arrangements existed to connect them when prepared with the serious conditions among our people in cities. For those who are working to remedy conditions in cities are not connected with a source of supply of capable recruits for social work.

Without delaying longer, some of us made a beginning to secure and train Negro college youth for Social work and to relate the Negro college to urban communities. The plan as started has three parts. First,

---

[*] From A. Johnson (Ed.), *Proceedings of the National Conference of Charities and Correction*, pp. 384–387. Fort Wayne, IN: Fort Wayne Printing Company, 1911.

the preparatory instruction and training in the Negro college; second, the selecting of promising students and providing them with the opportunities for further professional study and practical experience among their own people in cities; and third, the organization of social betterment work in the cities where these trained people may use their ability for social uplift.

First, the preparatory instruction and training of the students should be given in Negro colleges of the South because it should begin during college years of enthusiasm, and because it should be brought to bear upon the large groups of select, capable, enthusiastic Negro youth such as gather at these colleges. In this way prospective social workers may be found. Again, this preparation should begin in the Negro college, because the city conditions among Negroes demand minds and characters which have been moulded by a broad course of education.

Besides, some training for understanding the conditions surrounding my people should be put within the reach of all Negro college students. The problem of social uplift is so great that, in addition to expert social workers, all Negro ministers, doctors, lawyers, teachers, and others should have the benefit of instruction in scientific methods and the new social point of view. Finally and emphatically, the Negro colleges themselves need to be vitally articulated with the conditions and needs of the Negroes in the communities where these colleges are located. This will help the people and the students and show both the true aim of colleges.

With this in view, we have established at Fisk University, Nashville, Tenn., a department of Social Science and Social Work. In order to give a thorough preparation for social and religious workers, courses are given in industrial history, economic theory, sociology, economic and labor problems and methods of social work. In the Senior year lectures are given on special problems relating to Negroes. During the past school year lectures were given by experts from several cities on the religious problems among Negroes in cities; delinquents and probation problems; special problems of Negro women in cities; of Negro children; and on Principles of Relief. Running through half of the Junior year and all of the Senior year is a course in the History of the Negro in America and the Negro problem. This furnishes historical perspective and knowledge of the present condition of the Negro in America as seen from the points of view of various writers.

During the last semester of the Senior year, the students are required to give ten hours per week to methods of statistics and social investigations, and actual field work among the conditions of the colored people of Nashville. Thus we aim to bring the university into closer relation to our people in that city.

And this is just a beginning. We shall not confine our efforts to the students and graduates of Fisk University, but in a similar way we contemplate a general co-operation of Negro colleges for the betterment of the urban population of our people. However, Fisk University, by its strategic location in the South, by the way it looms up in the minds of Negroes themselves, by its standing among colleges of the country and by its tradition and sentiment for social service, is preeminently the place for the inception and development of such a movement.

Second, I turn to the selection of students of promise for Social Work and their further training in New York and other cities. A number of the leading white and colored citizens of New York, who wish to meet these urban problems, have organized the Committee on Urban Conditions Among Negroes. This Committee has three main purposes: First, to bring about co-operation among the existing agencies at work among Negroes in urban centers, to find out where additional work is needed and where existing work involves duplication; second, to make provision for discovered needs or to attempt otherwise to remedy the situation, and third, to secure and train Negro social workers.

To carry out the last named purpose, promising graduates of Fisk University and other colleges, who wish to make social work a life calling, will be given an opportunity under the auspices of this Committee to get experience in such social work and to pursue such further study as the social betterment efforts and educational facilities in New York and other cities afford.

We have a field-secretary in New York, who devotes his entire time to the Committee's work, and one of his special functions is to supervise the further training of these prospective social workers. This year, we have selected from two colleges, one graduate each. Our only limit in securing them was a lack of funds. These young people will be provided with fellowships that will afford opportunity for study at The New York School of Philanthropy and Columbia University.

The third part of the plan is the relation of these trained people to social betterment efforts in the cities. This is both cause and effect of the first two parts. In New York and other cities there is a persistent demand on the part of those doing and supporting social work, and a crying need among my people, that the many agencies for betterment shall be standardized and co-ordinated, and that efficient workers be secured and put in charge. We have begun to meet this need and demand. Last year, our Committee laid out the following five year program of work for New York City:

(1) Registration and co-operation of existing social agencies; (2) Co-operation of agencies at work for the improvement of the community at large; (3) Improvement of housing and neighborhood condi-

tions; (4) Development of employment agencies and facilities; (5) Development of thrift agencies and co-operative business enterprises; (6) Provision of amusement and recreation facilities; (7) Improvement in the relation of the Negro church and other religious institutions to the social conditions; (8) Co-operation with other cities in exchange of methods and in securing and training social workers.

Our resources have been very limited, but we have gathered and placed on file for reference, a reliable set of reports on eighteen of the existing agencies; in co-operation with the National League for the Protection of Colored Women, we made a preliminary survey of the largest Negro district in Manhattan. This resulted in a movement of the colored residents themselves for such improvements as better police protection and wholesome recreation and amusement facilities. We have under supervision arrangements for a model boy's camp and for co-operation of all Negro fresh-air agencies. Committees are appointed looking toward the union with us of two or three other important organizations to act as a general clearing house for the city. Workers in several other cities have signified their desire to join the movement.

Let me sum up this brief and fragmentary account of our plan: The urban concentration of Negroes demands a large number of trained Negro social workers. The usual way of securing and training them is to get any one who is available and to put him in charge of social work with the expectation that he will know by intuition and learn from failures to understand what are our most serious social conditions.

Now, if there is any one fact well known, it is that the Negro's situation cannot be helped by inefficient and inexperienced enthusiasts. Our committee goes back to the years of youth, the years of college enthusiasm for service, picks out the people of promise, insures them a good foundation training and gives them opportunity for further professional training and practical experience before entrusting such serious work into their hands.

The plan is feasible; our first year has succeeded beyond our hopes. It is meeting a need of the Negro college youth, and it is meeting the demand of those who have often lamented the lack of competent Negro workers. It is a new departure in the training of social workers, because it not only definitely links the training of the professional school for social workers with educational institutions of college rank, but also links the institutions and the students with a practical working committee, whose officers are to supervise the training of prospective social workers.

We believe firmly that, with financial support and co-operation, we shall give equipment and inspiration for social uplift to a number of capable Negro men and women; that we shall point the way for Negro colleges to articulate themselves with the increasing urban life; that we shall raise the standard and increase the efficiency of social betterment work among the urban Negro population of the country, and that we shall suggest some methods of connecting youth with the social problems which confront the Nation.

Forrester B. Washington
The Need and Education of Negro Social Workers*

Introduction

The attention of Negroes is focused on social work as a career at the present time as never before. Among the reasons for this interest are, *first*, the fact that a large proportion of the race is dependent for its very existence today on relief which is administered (theoretically, at least) by social workers, *second*, that the relief-administration phase of social work is the most available avenue of employment for college trained Negroes at the present time, and *third*, that considering the Negro in relation to the professions as a whole today, relief administration offers the larger and more certain salaries.

The Need of Negro Social Workers

The Negro People in America Face a Crisis

The Negro people are the chief sufferers in the United States today from the unemployment crisis and they have benefited less from the Recovery Program than the white group. These facts do not need to be argued. They are obvious, at least to all Negroes, and plenty of data are available to others who need to be convinced.

Only Social Workers Can Take Care of the Immediate Needs of These Distressed Negro People

This is not the place nor is there space here to enter into any lengthy discussion of the definition and goal of social work. It is sufficient for the purposes of this article to state that social work has been defined succinctly as "the adjustment of individuals and families to the environment in which they are living and conversely, the adjustment of the environment to the individual and the family."

When individuals or families get "out of step" with the orderly march of civilization—*i.e.*, unadjusted to their environment—social work takes charge. Modern social work was really called into being by the

---

* From *Journal of Negro Education*, 4 (January 1935), 76–93. Reprinted with permission.

tremendous changes in our economic and social life which made it increasingly difficult for large numbers of people to "keep in step." Industry has transferred masses of people from a rural to an urban environment and made them dependent on others for food, rent, and the like, where formerly they were self-sustaining.

When, therefore, industry breaks down, whether on a large or a small scale, and causes individual or mass unemployment, social work has to step in and take care of the "social problems" created, *i.e.*, those conditions or difficulties which cannot be handled by the individual concerned or the normal every-day institutions of society, such as the courts, the church, the school and the usual governmental bodies. Hence, the social worker has the relationship to the social organization and procedure that the mechanic has to machinery or the physician has to the body. This explains why it was that while business men, statesmen, and the learned professions were completely "flabbergasted" by the depression and did not know how to meet its onset, the social workers were ready with a program and knew how to put it into operation.

As has been indicated above, the Negroes of America are the worst victims, through no fault of their own, of the present economic crisis and because, as has also been indicated, it is at such times of economic dislocation that social work steps in to take care of the sufferers, the Negro is bound to be a major charge of the social-work group in America today....

Trained Social Workers Can Do the Job Much Better than Untrained Workers

[Real] progress has been made in social work only since it has been developed into a recognized profession. This development has been accomplished chiefly through the efforts of the training schools to systematize the various techniques used in social work so that they would be educationally communicable, to ascertain fundamental principles which applied to all forms of social work and to adapt scientific material to the needs of social work.

Trained social workers by the application of methods taught them in the schools have improved the techniques used in every type of social work. This is quite notable in emergency case work, where they have so reorganized the machinery of relief that it has much more adequately met the needs of unemployed families than in previous crises....

Negro Social Workers Can Accomplish More with Negro Clients than White Social Workers

The writer maintains that Negro workers can accomplish more with Negro clients than white workers. However, it cannot be taken for granted that this opinion is shared with him in every quarter. If it were left to Negro clients, their decision would probably be a "toss up" for there are many of them who state they prefer white workers. Likewise there are a number of social executives who profess to believe that white social workers are more successful with Negro clients than Negro workers....

The real test of course in the matter of white workers versus Negro workers in social work among Negroes is the question of who gets the best results. The facts are that the majority of agencies which have taken on Negro workers even before the depression did so after comparative studies of the length of time which it took Negroes and white workers to close the same type of Negro cases. They found more satisfactory adjustments made by the Negro worker and found that they were made in a shorter time. Of course this meant more real social service for their Negro clients and a saving in time and money for the agencies.

This discovery on the part of the agencies should not have been surprising. The Negro worker knows the resources of the Negro community better than the white worker. The Negro worker is in touch with the Negro community and is learning about it twenty-four hours per day while the white social worker leaves it at five o'clock when her day's work is ended. The white worker can not bring as much cooperation to her Negro cases from the Negro community as can the Negro worker. The white worker cannot get into the most intimate places of Negro life as can the Negro worker. The white worker's ignorance of the Negro community is dangerous because he or she has to make quick decisions and has little time and limited means for checking on homes and institutions to which she is referring Negroes in the Negro community....

If it is important to have a sympathetic understanding of everything which conditions the behavior of a client, then the white worker can never get the rapport with a Negro client which is possible to the Negro worker, because only the Negro worker can really know what it means to be a Negro. As long as there exists in this country such pronouncedly differential treatment of the Negro, it is obviously impossible to have real "transference," to borrow a psychoanalytical term, between a white worker and a Negro client. No matter what the white worker says or does, the Negro client will never come to the point of feeling absolutely certain of the white worker's attitude. There must be identification as between the client and worker for the latter to feel real security out of which there may develop real "transference." The white group has willed that such identification is not highly probable in this country....

There Is a Great Demand for Trained Negro Social Workers

The number of Negro social workers in the United States has increased tremendously since 1929. This has been due entirely to the large number of persons of both races who have been employed to administer relief, largely under public auspices, to the unemployed. As a matter of fact the numbers employed in practically all other forms of social work, and in private social work in general, has decreased. The experiences of the Negro social worker during the depression have followed closely those of the white except that the number of Negroes employed is less than his proportion in the general population in every community known to this writer. Nevertheless, the increase of Negroes in social work as a whole has been about 500 per cent, due entirely to the increase (about 1,000 per cent) in the number of Negroes in the case-work field. This latter increase in turn was due, as has been stated, almost entirely to the large number of Negroes employed in the public-relief field during the current economic crisis.

While the demand for Negro workers still exists it has changed in two ways since the tremendous over-night hiring of relief workers as the various Emergency Relief Administrations were being set up.

The communities which first decided to use Negro workers, usually cities with the largest Negro populations, are now pretty well staffed. The present requisitions for Negro workers are coming largely from smaller communities where public opinion seems heretofore to have resisted the employment of Negro workers. Moreover, the type sought has changed from those with a college education to those with formal training in social work plus a college education....

Although the Atlanta School of Social Work, which specializes in the training of Negroes for the profession, has greatly increased its facilities for absorbing students and has doubled its enrollment this year over last year (1933-1934) and has five times the enrollment it had in the year previous to the depression, nevertheless, it is still unable to supply the requests for graduates....

The Education of the Negro Social Worker

It should not really be necessary to argue the value of general training for social work (as distinguished from training of those who will do social work among Negroes). The value of social-work training as a general proposition has been hinted at already in this article.

Briefly the value of social-work training might be summed up as follows: It enables the student to learn the various techniques and skills which have been developed by those people who have been compelled to treat the social problems which have evolved as society has become more complex. There are so many of these skills or techniques that it would be practically impossible for anyone to learn all of them by working first in one agency and then another. It is necessary that they be boiled down, coordinated, integrated and presented in a school just as it was necessary for the various types of legal procedure to be similarly organized for the efficient learning of law....

Above all, professional training in social work teaches us that we are living in a changing world and in a world which is changing at a faster rate all the time. Training teaches us that social progress is becoming more and more complex. It keeps us from accepting any fixed idea of an established system of social work. We are willing to try new ideas which will be for the betterment of the human race. We accept no old ideas as gospel. The trained social worker knows that social work expands from time to time and that many present-day social work functions in the past were not considered as social work at all.

Only by formal training can one be prepared, in addition to carrying on remedial and preventive social work, to plan a new and better society. Right now our attentions should be concentrated on those phases of social planning which are mutually related to the great human quest for added security....

Desirable Candidates

The type of Negro candidate entering social work has gone through some interesting developments during the last twenty years. In the South, particularly, before the establishment of the Atlanta School of Social Work there was a marked tendency to employ untrained Negro social workers whereas the same agency would not employ untrained white workers. This occurred in the South for various reasons among which are the following: Not many trained Negroes were available; social executives were not so particular about the quality of social work done among Negroes as among whites; agencies did not intend to spend as much money on Negro clients as whites (and a trained worker would cost more than an untrained worker); social executives did not, in many cases, like educated Negroes of any kind because they had to treat them too respectfully; and, finally, social executives were inclined to hire the relatives of some cook or chauffeur or even the cook or chauffeur himself.

But this tendency in the earlier days to employ untrained Negro workers was not entirely confined to the South. It occurred also in the North for various reasons. Among these were the same scarcity of trained Negro workers, the same lack of concern about the quality of work done among Negroes, and the same desire to economize in the case of Negro clients through the use of inferior workers. Moreover, in the North also, some of the pioneer Negro executives in social work were inclined to favor their friends when it came to staff appointments rather than to seek trained Negroes. Some of the pioneer Negro executives also had a great tendency toward attempting to please the local Negro community by making appointments of home-town talent, irrespective of the amount of training the latter possessed.

Fortunately, social work among Negroes is getting away from this old-time tendency. There are several reasons for this. In both the North and the South the advent of better-trained persons to executive positions in the agencies was followed frequently by staff "house-cleanings" wherein both untrained white and colored workers were displaced by trained persons. In the South the rapid spread of the influence of the Atlanta School of Social Work undoubtedly had some effect. From year to year the Atlanta School of Social Work has offered an increasing number of trained Negroes to Southern social agencies. In addition it has raised its entrance requirements from that of high school graduation or less to a point where now it will accept no one with less than two years of college training, and actually gives preference to college graduates of whom its present student body now largely consists....

Even a higher grade of material is needed for training for social work among Negroes than is true for social work among white people. Those who are to do social work among Negroes need to know everything which is needed by those who work among whites and then considerably more....

Fortunately, judging from the experiences of the Atlanta School of Social Work we are not only able to select from a much larger group of Negro candidates for training than heretofore, but from a much better group. Perhaps it is a good thing that the attention of college-bred Negroes is being turned toward social work as a career to an extent that was never true before....

It is undoubtedly a good thing that we are having, as a result of the leveling processes which are accompanying the present economic crisis, a trek into the social work profession of Negro men and women of higher calibre intellectually as well as from the point of view of personality. They will give better leadership in social work among Negroes in the future....

General Training at Schools of Social Work

Just as there are many individual Negroes at the present time endeavoring to obtain training for social work simply because it seems to be a lucrative "racket" so there are many Negro colleges trying to get into the business of social-work training because of motives not much more laudable than those of the individuals cited. Some of the colleges which have attempted to launch such projects have undoubtedly been motivated with a sincere desire to meet the great need for trained Negro social workers and some of them have honestly intended to meet every one of the standards set up by the American Association of Schools of Social Work. But these standards are necessarily high. The establishment of a school of social work is expensive and its operation is expensive. Consequently, there is a great temptation to set these new curricula in motion whether the standards are met or not.

In communities where Negroes are not admitted to existing local schools of social work because of racial segregation there has been in a number of cases a tendency to inveigle Negroes into "fly-by-night" schemes of social work training. In 1928 in an article in Hospital Social Service (Vol. XVII), E. Franklin Frazier called attention to the fact that Negroes were in danger of becoming the victims of the institute method of learning social work. "After this method was more or less abandoned in the South for white people it was revived for the social work training of Negroes," writes Mr. Frazier.

At the present time there is danger of a revival of this same situation to which Frazier called attention several years ago. In certain localities where white workers have been sent away by some public or private agency to be trained at accredited schools of social work, Negro workers connected with the same agencies have been provided with only a week or two of institute training.

Negroes who intend to make social work a career should be very careful to connect themselves with reputable institutions for training because if they do not they will be wasting their time, money, and energy in the long run. The better private social-work agencies will only employ persons who are eligible for membership in the American Association of Social Workers and the latter organization no longer accepts members who have not graduated from accredited schools of social work, in other words, from one of the 27 schools which are members of the American Association of Schools of Social Work....

Existing schools of social work are doing everything in their power to increase their ability to absorb more pupils. It is reasonable to suppose that it is easier and less expensive to increase the opportunities for training through expanding existing schools than by setting up new schools. The New York School of Social Work, the oldest member of the Association of Schools of Social Work, has increased its enrollment this year to a record number of 710. The Atlanta School of Social Work, which is the only Negro school in the Association, has doubled its enrollment this year over last year and has a student body which is five times as large as the year just before the depression began....

Special Training for Social Work among Negroes

There is no such thing as "Negro social work" (biologically speaking). But this writer maintains that "social work among Negroes" has some points of departure from social work among white people other than the fact that it is done among people of a different color. This concept of a special departure of social work among Negroes from the norm has grown out of a thoughtful consideration of the experiences of persons, mostly Negroes, who have been engaged for many years in social work with the group.

There are many special problems and many types of social action with which persons about to enter social work among Negroes ought to be acquainted but with which in most cases unfortunately they do not become familiar until after they are on the job....

It is the writer's belief, which he is attempting to carry out at the Atlanta School of Social Work, that specialized training for persons who are to do social work among Negroes is necessary for several reasons. Specialized training is necessary, first, to get a perspective of the broader problems of the Negro's adjustment to life; to understand that the Negro has to make a triple adjustment to life, not only to the ordinary "work-a-day" world to which everyone has to adjust but secondly to a world of discrimination and segregation, and thirdly, to a Negro world in which competition for trivialities takes on great importance. It is necessary to have specialized training to avoid the mistakes which have been made in the past in social work among Negroes; to protect the helpless Negro client from becoming the victim of futile experimentation and to avoid the waste of time and energy in the "trial and error" method. It has taken many of the pioneers in social work among Negroes ten or fifteen years to learn all of the substitute mechanisms that are necessary to successfully carry on social work programs among Negroes. The organization and conversion of the experiences of these "old timers" into teaching material has made it possible for graduates of the Atlanta School of Social Work to learn in two years what it has taken the pioneers a decade or more to learn, and in addition has enabled these graduates to do more than their predecessors in the same length of time in the same field.

The type of training we are discussing here should prepare workers in the Negro community to look for and detect changing phases in Negro group life. It should enable the worker to know whether agencies carrying on social work among Negroes have been stressing too much or too long certain types of programs. It should answer the question as to whether social workers among Negroes are, for instance, overemphasizing the physical factors and neglecting the psychological factors, and whether certain types of social work among Negroes have become outmoded, and whether concern for the migration phase of Negro life has been continued too long and whether there is not something even more fundamental than that which underlies the industrial phase, and finally, whether the time is not ripe for a shift in social work among Negroes from emphasis on philanthropy to emphasis on group life and survival.

The Jews know to which stage they have arrived in social work in America, but do Negroes? We cannot know this without training, without being able to review understandingly the stages through which all society has come, and more especially the minority groups. The Jews claim they have passed their adolescent period in social work in the United States of America, but has the Negro? The writer does not think so. It is his opinion that those of us who are seriously interested in improving the Negro's condition through social work must look about ourselves and scrutinize much more intently what has happened to the Negro. What we discover (our shortcomings and gaps in the social work program for Negroes) will shock and hurt us undoubtedly, but we must know the real situation. Only by training can we know what to look for and what can be done....

If we are to have an ideal form of training for persons going into social work among Negroes, specialized courses such as have been indicated here must be included. The writer realizes that many social workers among Negroes do not agree with him. He also realizes that non-racial schools cannot be expected to offer such specialized training. That is why the Jews started a school of social work of their own. The majority group cannot be expected to be interested in the minority group *per se* or in social-work courses that have as their special objective the survival of certain minority groups. It is obvious that the only place these courses can be expected to be obtained is in a school that devotes itself solely to the training of Negroes for social work....

Conclusion

Only on such a broad basis as the writer has outlined should Negroes be trained for social work. The writer wishes to reemphasize this thesis that in training Negroes for social work it is more important than is true of other groups that they be trained for social planning as well as social work. A real minority-group strategy is the thing the Negro group in America needs....

Social-work training is the only training which can provide the leadership for the social planning herein indicated. Almost any other type of training would have to be revamped from the bottom up, to provide the kind of leadership which the Negro now needs.

It is too much to expect that individuals outside of the Negro group will dedicate themselves to this type of program. Moreover, while social work in some of its aspects, particularly relief, will be taken over in an increasing degree by the state, it is ridiculous to expect that the state will, within any reasonable time, take upon itself particular programs for the adjustment and advancement of the Negro or any other minority group. Certainly this will not be true in those sections where Negroes need these programs most.

4. The Relationship between Social Work Training and the Development of a Profession

> Is social work a profession in the...strict sense of the term?...I have made the point that all the established and recognized professions have definite and specific ends....This is not true of social work. It appears not so much a definite field as an aspect of work in many fields.
>
> Abraham Flexner, 1915

Virtually every article or book ever written on social work professionalism begins the discussion with a reference to Abraham Flexner's famous speech before the National Conference of Charities and Correction in 1915. Flexner titled his address simply "Is Social Work a Profession?" His carefully argued "No" has reverberated through the decades of social work's subsequent development. Flexner's reasoning and conclusions have been used to explain social work's stress on an individualized, often psychiatrically-oriented casework method rather than social reform and to help illuminate the field's "obsession" with professional status (see Ehrenreich, 1985, pp. 56-59; Lubove, 1969, pp. 106-107; Specht & Courtney, 1994, pp. 86–88). Yet while Flexner's analysis has undoubtedly been one of the influences on the ways in which social work has sought to legitimize itself as a profession, the notion that his message devastated its national conference audience seems overblown. What seems more likely is that the conference leadership invited Flexner to speak specifically because his approach would support their own ideas about the ways to strengthen social work.

When the conference planners chose Flexner to address the issue of social work's status as a profession, they were asking the advice of a person nationally known for his expertise in evaluating professional education and standards. Flexner, the assistant secretary of the General Education Board of New York City and widely regarded as an authority on graduate professional education, had earlier carried out an evaluation of medical education commissioned by the American

Medical Association. His report led to a radical weeding out of smaller, less well-financed medical schools (Flexner, 1910; Starr, 1982). Social workers were once again looking to a medical model of professional status, but, for good measure, they added to the conference panel the prominent Harvard lawyer, Felix Frankfurter, who would later become a Supreme Court Justice.

Flexner's speech makes a number of points about social work which remain relevant today. Social work educators, students, and practitioners who despair of coming up with an answer to the question "What is social work?" will appreciate his description of the extraordinary breadth of the field. Flexner notes the difficulty of developing an education program that can encompass all aspects of social work in a meaningful way. Looking at the range of social work positions described in material from the Boston School of Social Work, he remarks that "the field of employment is indeed so vast that delimitation is impossible." Interestingly, despite the difficulties in building a coherent curriculum in social work education, advocates of professionalization would soon come to see professional education as a common base for cohesion, and the graduate degree as a confirmation of an individual's professional status. As Walter West, executive director of the American Association of Social Workers, put it in 1930:

> Schools of social work are one of the major things you can offer as evidence that social work has a meaning in practice....It's a shortcut to a person to whom you can't tell or demonstrate the competence of social workers. (Leighninger, 1987, p. 38)

Abraham Flexner

Assistant Secretary, General Education Board, New York City

Is Social Work a Profession?*

Before beginning to consider whether social work is or is not a profession, I must confess a very genuine doubt as to my competency to undertake the discussion. My acquaintance with social work, with the literature of social work, and with social workers is distinctly limited,—far too much so. Hence if the conclusions that I have reached seem to you unsound or academic, I beg you to understand that I should not be disposed to press them....

I have not been asked to decide whether social work is a full-time or a part-time occupation, whether, in a word, it is a professional or an amateur occupation....The question put to me is a more technical one. The term profession, strictly used, as opposed to business or handicraft, is a title of peculiar distinction, coveted by many activities. Thus far it has been pretty indiscriminately used. Almost any occupation not obviously a business is apt to classify itself as a profession. Doctors, lawyers, preachers, musicians, engineers, journalists, trained nurses, trapeze and dancing masters, equestrians, and chiropodists—all speak of their *profession.* Their claims are supposed to be established beyond question if they are able to affix to their names one of those magical combinations of letters that either are or look like an academic degree....

But to make a profession in the genuine sense, something more than a mere claim or an academic degree is needed. There are certain objective standards that can be formulated. Social work is interested in being recognized as a profession only if the term is limited to activities possessing these criteria. The social worker wants, I assume, to be a professional, if at all, only in the sense in which the physician and the engineer are professional, and he wants to make common cause with them in defending the term against deterioration. In this narrower and eulogistic sense, what are the earmarks of a profession?...

The definition that we may formulate today will therefore need recasting from time to time, and internal modifications will occur in

---

* From *Proceedings of the National Conference of Charities and Correction,* pp. 575–590. Chicago: Hildmann Printing Company, 1915.

many of the activities that we shall mention. My present concern, however, is not to consider the evolutionary aspects of the problem, but rather to ask what are at this moment the criteria of a profession and to consider whether social work conforms to them. There are a few professions universally admitted to be such,—law, medicine, and preaching. From these one must by analysis extract the criteria with which, at least, one must begin the characterization of professions. As we proceed, we shall consider how far the conception has been widened or modified by the addition of new professions; and finally, to what extent social work measures up to the standard thus reached.

Would it not be fair to mention as the first mark of a profession that the activities involved are essentially intellectual in character?...A free, resourceful, and unhampered intelligence applied to problems and seeking to understand and master them,—that is in the first instance characteristic of a profession.

Wherever intelligence plays thus freely, the responsibility of the practitioner is at once large and personal. The problems to be dealt with are complicated; the facilities at hand, more or less abundant and various; the agent—physician, engineer, or preacher—exercises a very large discretion as to what he shall do. He is not under orders; though he be cooperating with others, though the work be team work, rather than individual work, his responsibility is not less complete and not less personal. This quality of responsibility follows from the fact that professions are intellectual in character; for in all intellectual operations, the thinker takes upon himself a risk....

Professions would fall short of attaining intellectuality if they employed mainly or even largely knowledge and experience that is generally accessible,—if they drew, that is, only on the usual available sources of information. They need to resort to the laboratory and the seminar for a constantly fresh supply of facts; and it is the steady stream of ideas, emanating from sources, which keeps professions from degenerating into mere routine, from losing their intellectual and responsible character. The second criterion of the profession is therefore its learned character, and this characteristic is so essential that the adjective *learned* really adds nothing to the noun profession.

Professions are therefore intellectual and learned; they are in the next place definitely practical. No profession can be merely academic and theoretic; the professional man must have an absolutely definite and practical object. His processes are essentially intellectual; his raw material is derived from the world of learning; thereupon he must do with it a clean-cut, concrete task. All the activities about the professional quality of which we should at once agree are not only intellectual and learned, but definite in purpose. The professions of law, medicine, architecture, and engineering, for example, operate within definite fields and strive towards objects capable of clear, unambiguous, and concrete formulation....

Each of the unmistakable professions already mentioned for the purpose of illustration possesses a technique capable of communication through an orderly and highly specialized educational discipline. Despite differences of opinion about details, the members of a given profession are pretty well agreed as to the specific objects that the profession seeks to fulfill, and the specific kinds of skill that the practitioner of the profession must master in order to attain the object in question. On this basis, men arrive at an understanding as to the amount and quality of training, general and special, which should precede admission into the professional school; as to the content and length of the professional course. These formulations are meant to exclude from professions those incapable of pursuing them in a large, free, and responsible way; and to make sure that those potentially capable are so instructed as to get the fullest possible benefit from the training provided.

A profession is a brotherhood,—almost, if the word could be purified of its invidious implications, a caste. Professional activities are so definite, so absorbing in interest, so rich in duties and responsibilities, that they completely engage their votaries. The social and personal lives of professional men and of their families thus tend to organize around a professional nucleus. A strong class consciousness soon develops....

There is, of course, always danger that the interests of an organization may conflict with those of the body politic. Organizations of physicians, lawyers, and teachers may find the personal interests of the individuals of whom they are composed arrayed against those of society at large. On the whole, however, organized groups of this kind are, under democratic conditions, apt to be more responsive to public interest than are unorganized and isolated individuals. In any event, under the pressure of public opinion, professional groups have more and more tended to view themselves as organs contrived for the achievement of social ends rather than as bodies formed to stand together for the assertion of rights or the protection of interests and principles. I do not wish to be understood as saying that this development is as yet by any means complete. Such is far from being the case. Organizations of teachers, doctors, and lawyers are still apt to look out, first of all, for "number one." But as time goes on it may very well come to be a mark of professional character that the professional organization is explicitly and admittedly meant for the advancement of the common social interest through the professional organization. Devotion to well-doing is thus more and more likely to become an accepted mark of professional activity; and as this development proceeds, the pecuniary interest of the individual practitioner of a given profession is apt to yield gradually before an increasing realization of responsibility to a larger end.

Let me now review briefly the six criteria which we have mentioned: professions involve essentially intellectual operations with large individual responsibility; they derive their raw material from science and learning; this material they work up to a practical and definite end; they possess an educationally communicable technique; they tend to self-organization; they are becoming increasingly altruistic in motivation. It will be interesting to submit various forms of activity to the test in order to determine whether these criteria work....

Is trained nursing a profession?...I am conscious of endeavoring to pick up a live wire when I undertake to determine the status of the trained nurse. But if consideration of various activities serially arranged will throw any light upon the problem as related to the social worker, there are obvious advantages in discussing the twilight cases. The trained nurse is making a praiseworthy and important effort to improve the status of her vocation. She urges, and with justice, that her position is one of great responsibility; that she must possess knowledge, skill, and power of judgment; that the chances of securing these qualifications, all of them essentially intellectual, improve, as the occupation increases in dignity. It is to be observed, however, that the responsibility of the trained nurse is neither original nor final. She, too, may be described as another arm to the physician or surgeon. Her function is instrumental, though not, indeed, just mechanically instrumental. In certain relations she is perhaps almost a collaborator. Yet, when all is said, it is the physician who observes, reflects, and decides. The trained nurse plays into his hands; carries out his orders; summons him like a sentinel in fresh emergencies; subordinates loyally her intelligence to his theory, to his policy, and is effective in precise proportion to her ability thus to second his efforts. Can an activity of this secondary nature be deemed a profession? On the answer, an entire educational policy depends....

With medicine, law, engineering, literature, painting, music, we emerge from all clouds of doubt into the unmistakable professions. Without exception, these callings involve personally responsible intellectual activity; they derive their material immediately from learning and science; they possess an organized and educationally communicable technique; they have evolved into definite status, social and professional, and they tend to become, more and more clearly, organs for the achievement of large social ends. I need not establish this position separately in reference to each of them. Let the case of medicine suffice. The physician's function is overwhelmingly intellectual in quality and his responsibility absolutely personal. He utilizes various instruments, physical and human: microscope, stethoscope, sphygmograph, orderly, pharmacist, dietician, nurse. But his is the commanding intelligence that brings these resources to bear; his is the responsibility of decision as to the problem and how it is to be solved....

Medicine qualifies on other points equally well: it has the definite, practical end already noted, viz: the preservation and restoration of health; it lends itself admirably to an effective and orderly educational discipline, calculated to obtain the definite object just stated; it has achieved a very definite status; finally, though neither the organization as a whole nor the members as individuals can claim to be exempt from selfish and mercenary motives, it must in fairness be said that the medical profession has shown a genuine regard for the public interest as against its own, that it is increasingly responsive to large social needs, and that there are not wanting signs of a development that will minimize personal profit somewhat as it is minimized in teaching.

I hope that these examples have made our criteria so clear that they can now be applied to social work. Is social work a profession in the technical and strict sense of the term? The Bulletin of the New York School of Philanthropy under the title *The Profession of Social Work* makes the following explanation:

> The School of Philanthropy is primarily a professional training school, of graduate rank, for civic and social work. The word *philanthropy* is to be understood in the broadest and deepest sense as including every kind of social work, whether under public or private auspices. By social work is meant any form of persistent and deliberate effort to improve living or working conditions in the community, or to relieve, diminish, or prevent distress, whether due to weakness of character or to pressure of external circumstances. All such efforts may be conceived as falling under the heads of charity, education, or justice, and the same action may sometime appear as one or another according to the point of view.

The activities described in these words are obviously intellectual, not mechanical, not routine in character. The worker must possess fine powers of analysis and discrimination, breadth and flexibility of sympathy, sound judgment, skill in utilizing whatever resources are available, facility in devising new combinations. These operations are assuredly of intellectual quality.

I confess I am not clear, however, as to whether this responsibility is not rather that of mediating than the original agency....Let me explain as concretely as I can. The engineer works out his problem and puts through its solution; so does the physician, the preacher, the teacher. The social worker takes hold of a case, that of a disintegrating family, a wrecked individual, or an unsocialized industry. Having localized his problem, having decided on its particular nature, is he not usually driven to invoke the specialized agency, professional or other, best equipped to handle it? There is illness to be dealt with—the doctor is needed; ignorance requires the school; poverty calls for the legislator, organized charity, and so on. To the extent that the social worker mediates the intervention of the particular agent or agency best fitted to deal with the specific emergency which he has encountered, is the social worker himself a professional or is he the intelligence that brings this or that profession or other activity into action? The responsibility for specific action thus rests upon the power he has invoked. The very variety of the situations he encounters compels him to be not a professional agent so much as the mediator invoking this or that professional agency....

Consideration of the objects of social work leads to the same conclusion. I have made the point that all the established and recognized professions have definite and specific ends: medicine, law, architecture, engineering—one can draw a clear line of demarcation about their respective fields. This is not true of social work. It appears not so much a definite field as an aspect of work in many fields. An aspect of medicine belongs to social work, as do certain aspects of law, education, architecture, etc. Recur for a moment to the scope of interest indicated in the abstract above quoted from the prospectus of the New York School: the improvement of living and working conditions in the community, the relief or prevention of distress whether individual or social in origin. The prospectus of the Boston School for Social Workers enumerates the various kinds of positions occupied by its graduates as follows: care of children, church and religious work, civic agencies, industrial betterment, institutional and medical social service, neighborhood work and recreation, organizing charity, probation and parole. The field of employment is indeed so vast that delimitation is impossible....

Lack of specificity in aim affects seriously the problem of training social workers. Professions that are able to define their objects precisely can work out educational procedures capable of accomplishing a desired result. But the occupations of social workers are so numerous and diverse that no compact, purposefully organized educational discipline is feasible. Well-informed, well-balanced, tactful, judicious, sympathetic, resourceful people are needed, rather than any definite kind or kinds of technical skill. In so far as education can produce this type, the education is not technically professional so much as broadly cultural in a variety of realms of civic and social interest. The vagueness of the enterprise in which they are engaged must have troubled the instructors themselves, if I may judge from a remark once made to me by one of them: "We don't know just what to teach them." In this connection it is worth noting that the heads of schools for social workers are trained men with subsequent experience, but not trained social workers. Dr. Graham Taylor is a theologian by training, Dr. Brackett and Dr. Devine are economists. In addition to knowing a specialty well, they are all well-informed in many other directions. This breadth of interest and attainment reinforced by practical experience makes them competent heads of schools for social workers—this, rather than any particular training aimed at the particular job.

Let me add, however, that what I have just said does not imply that schools of philanthropy are superfluous. Looking at them as educational ventures, I suspect that they are as yet feeling about for their proper place and function. There is an obvious convenience, however, in having an institution which focuses as far as possible the main lines of social activity; an obvious advantage in having an institution that emphasizes the practical side of what might otherwise be more or less academic instruction in many branches. But instruction of this kind is not exactly professional in character; it supplements and brings to bear what good students might well acquire in the course of their previous higher education.

If social work fails to conform to some professional criteria, it very readily satisfies others. No question can be raised as to the source from which the social worker derives his material—it comes obviously from science and learning, from economics, ethics, religion and medicine; nor is there any doubt on the score of the rapid evolution of a professional self-consciousness, as these annual conferences abundantly testify. Finally, in the one respect in which most professions still fall short, social work is fairly on the same level as education, for the rewards of the social worker are in his own conscience and in heaven. His life is marked by devotion to impersonal ends and his own satisfaction is largely through the satisfactions procured by his efforts for others....

Now that we have run through the marks of the professions and have found that on the whole at this stage social work is hardly eligible, it is fair to ask whether we have not been simply engaged in verbal quibbling. Has an analysis of this kind any practical significance?

It seems to me that it has. For example: the social worker is at times perhaps somewhat too self-confident; social work has suffered to some extent from one of the vices associated with journalism, excessive facility in speech and in action. Let us suppose for a moment that our reflection on the differences between the accepted professions and social work reminds the social worker at crucial moments that he is, as social worker, not so much an expert himself as the mediator whose concern it is to summon the expert: will not his observation be calmer, his utterance more restrained, be the difficulty he encounters economic, educational, or sanitary? He will, I mean, be conscious of his dependence, and this consciousness will tend to induce caution, thoroughness, and moderation. For if social work is not definite enough to be called a profession, the social worker will at least be less cock-sure than the professional man whom he calls in....

At the moment, therefore, it may be—observe that I am not endeavoring to be very positive—it may be that social work will gain if it becomes uncomfortably conscious that it is not a profession in the sense in which medicine and engineering are professions; that if medicine and engineering have cause to proceed with critical care, social work has even more....

But, after all, what matters most is professional spirit. All activities may be prosecuted in the genuine professional spirit. In so far as accepted professions are prosecuted at a mercenary or selfish level, law and medicine are ethically no better than trades. In so far as trades are honestly carried on, they tend to rise towards the professional level. Social work appeals strongly to the humanitarian and spiritual element. It holds out no inducement to the worldly—neither comfort, glory, nor money. The unselfish devotion of those who have chosen to give themselves to making the world a fitter place to live in can fill social work with the professional spirit and thus to some extent lift it above all the distinctions which I have been at such pains to make. In the long run, the first, main and indispensable criterion of a profession will be the possession of professional spirit, and that test social work may, if it will, fully satisfy.

Edward T. Devine's article "A Profession in the Making," appeared in the social work journal *The Survey* one year after Flexner's speech. It serves as a good example of social work's determination to move forward in developing itself as a useful profession. Aware of the kind of diversity within the field described by Flexner, Devine calls for social work's unification as a "common family." A key figure in the early years of the Charity Organization movement, Devine headed the NY Charity Organization Society and edited the movement's journal, *Charities*. He also served as a director of the New York School of Social Work. Although Devine at first subscribed to the charity movement's stress on individual casework, he, like Mary Richmond, soon saw the need for social reform. Thus he believed that an important feature of the social work family was the interrelationship between social workers in relief societies and those promoting improved housing, medical care, and other forms of institutional change.

Edward T. Devine
A Profession in the Making*

The social spirit in America has expressed itself variously as organized charity, housing and public health movements, settlements, municipal procedure and prison reform, playgrounds and recreation centers, religious and medical social service, industrial commissions and public welfare departments.

These diversified and yet, in essential aim and motive, closely allied activities, have given rise to a new vocation, to a profession in the making. This calling, from the very nature of the work to be done in it, and from the character of its leaders, makes an extraordinary appeal to the missionary spirit of the young men and women, in and out of the universities, who have seen the vision of a new social order in which poverty, crime and disease, if not wholly abolished, will certainly be vastly diminished, and will not exist, at any rate, as the result of social neglect, as the result of bad traditions which enlightenment can end, or of obsolete institutions which the laws can change.

These allied activities of the new social reform have caught up and, as it were, assimilated many of the old established agencies for relieving individual distress and misfortune. The hospital is no longer merely a refuge for the sick but also a health center. From it radiate prevention and educational influences as important as the bedside ministrations to the sick. The orphan asylum is no longer a place to keep a few orphans alive, but a child welfare station, in which the whole problem of organizing the educational, moral, economic and recreational life of the child may be studied, in some respects even better than in the necessarily more complex normal home life. The relief society is no longer solely to supply food and fuel and clothing to the "worthy poor," but is to improve their condition, to re-establish their earning capacity and independence. For these reasons, the men and women who are employed in relief societies, children's institutions, and hospitals find themselves wholly akin to the social workers who are securing new housing and compensation laws, promoting instructive nursing and medical inspection, or revising a discredited penal system.

A few of the older agencies and a few that are mediaeval in spirit, even if recently founded, have been left behind in this new alignment of social forces, but speaking generally it is certainly true that the so-called charitable activities of the country are faced in the forward direction; that their desire is not merely to help individuals, but to im-

---

* From *The Survey*, January 1, 1916, 403–410.

prove the conditions of life; that they think of themselves as social, educational and preventive agencies, and would have no sympathy with but only abhorrence for the notion that it is desirable to maintain a class of "deserving poor" in order that there may be some one on whom to lavish our bounty....

The things which the social workers do in common—their difficulties, obstacles and discouragements, their purposes, ideals and achievements—unite them in a common family in spite of great differences in their training and education, in their specific duties, in their relations with their respective employers, in the extent to which they have independent professional responsibility on their own shoulders, in the permanence of their tenure and even in the compensation for similar service.

Such a consciousness of common interests has usually come in the past either through some quasi-legal monopoly such as exists in the practice of law and medicine, through a class guild or trade union movement. Social work has no protection of academic professional degree or public examination, and it has no union or association to protect the economic interests of its members....

The time has come when social workers themselves, not through trade union or monopoly methods, but through methods now considered appropriate and rational in other professions, may advantageously give more attention to the question of thorough preparation for their chosen career. As a contribution to an understanding of the present situation the Intercollegiate Bureau of Occupations and the School of Philanthropy have made a study of present positions in social work in New York City....From the organizations and from individual social workers the facts have been gleaned in regard to salaries, education and training, length of service and duties of those who are employed in the voluntary social agencies....Many of them receive exceedingly small salaries, and many of them, not always necessarily the same ones, have little general education, and so little special training, that their presence can be accounted for only by the absence of effective competition or by very low standards in their employers. In many instances the societies could well afford to increase salaries if competent and expert workers could then be found to accept them....

It is evident that not highly trained specialists in a hundred different specialized fields, but thoroughly trained experts in the broader aspects of social work are most in demand, and that as such available experts increase in number, some of those now employed must necessarily give way. This is in the public interest and especially in the interest of those who need relief or service and for whose sake the agencies came into existence. As the requirements of social work are raised, professional training becomes more necessary and salaries must be correspondingly increased to cover this cost of preparation. This is just what is taking place.

The professional school not only serves those who enter it, by giving them a grounding in the principles, methods and history of social work; it serves also by a selective process the agencies who engage social workers. There are those who are especially fitted for social work. It is a part of the task of the professional school to discover such persons and to persuade them to enter it. There are others who, whatever their gifts and fitness for other occupations, are not fitted for social work. It is a part of the professional school to help them at an early stage to discover their limitations and thus to save a waste of their own time and resources, and to save the social agencies a needless disappointment. The school will not be infallible in this process and the way will always be open for persistent candidates to find their own opportunity for a demonstration of what they can do. The school, however, will naturally be on the eager search for all promising men and women and will have its greatest satisfaction in the discovery and development of those who "to natural ability and talents" add "the systematic training and theoretical knowledge to be gained from education, so that "there results a personality of unusual force and value" ...

Ignorant, incompetent and untrained employees of social agencies should be gradually, and not too gradually, displaced by trained and capable workers. Those already at work who are not too old to learn and who are capable of learning should be encouraged to take special extension courses at a school for training social workers or elsewhere. Executives who are responsible for engaging the staff should get out of their heads the dreary platitudes about "personality" and "natural gifts," and cooperate with the universities and training schools in uniting "ability and talents" to "systematic training." Boards of directors should make up their minds to pay adequate salaries to workers already competent.

The training schools on their part should undertake to meet the actual needs, setting the standards for admission and graduation neither so low as to betray the profession which they are helping to create, nor so high as to fail to provide workers who can afford to accept the positions which exist....[Social workers], if they fully realize their own professional obligations and become fully conscious of their responsibilities, may establish standards of preparation, of promotion and tenure, of compensation and security against both personal misfortune and failure to be of the greatest possible service in their own calling— all of which will be of direct and substantial value to their employers, to those under their care and to the public.

5. The Shape of the Emerging Professional Education for Social Work

> Students who have had, in the college or university, courses dealing with the causes of poverty or with social politics or similar subjects may have learned why social work is being done. The courses in the school of philanthropy teach how it is done or how it ought to be done.
>
> Edith Abbott

By 1915, the future shape of social work education was becoming apparent. In that year, Bryn Mawr College established what was probably the first completely graduate-level school of social work (Coohey, 1999). The New York School, under the leadership of Porter Lee, was rapidly moving toward its signature focus on a technique-based casework curriculum and a skills-oriented definition of social work. Lee, the former director of the Philadelphia Charity Organization Society, helped the school develop specialized tracks in medical, family, child, and eventually, psychiatric social work. Similar to today's schools, the New York School offered a year of foundation work, followed by a year of specialization (Dore, 1999; Shoemaker, 1998). The Chicago School of Civics and Philanthropy was still under Graham Taylor's direction, and still free of university affiliation. Yet by 1920 Edith Abbott and Sophonisba Breckinridge, who worked in the school's research department, had taken control of the school and negotiated its affiliation with the University of Chicago. Under Abbott and Breckinridge's leadership, the new School of Social Service Administration would fast create a reputation for preparing students for research, administrative, and policy positions, particularly in the growing arena of public welfare (Costin, 1983).

Few schools followed the School of Social Service Administration approach; the casework focus of the New York School was far more common. Yet elements of both emphases would come to be reflected in the social work curriculum. And as we see in the following selections, many of what are now standard aspects of professional social work education were falling into place.

Edith Abbott's article, "Education for Social Work," shows the breadth of her knowledge about social work and her commitment to the professionalization of this new field. This commitment was clear in her later work as the first Dean of the School of Social Service Administration and in her leadership positions in the American Association of Schools of Social Work. Abbott's fervor can be attributed in part to her experience as a well-educated middle-class woman at a time when few professional careers were open to women. Edith and her sister Grace came from a small town in Nebraska. Their father held a state political office and their mother had been a school principal. From their parents, the sisters inherited a strong commitment to education, women's rights, and progressive ideas. Edith studied at the London School of Economics and received a Ph.D. in economics at the University of Chicago in 1905. Grace, more an activist than a scholar, received a master's degree in political science. Yet both women faced a paucity of formal career paths that would make use of their education and skills.

The Abbotts gravitated to Jane Addams's Hull House, where Edith found a role as a researcher in the areas of housing conditions of the poor, the situation of working women, juvenile delinquency, and child labor. While Grace took the path of an activist, first heading an organization set up to prevent exploitation of immigrants, and later becoming the chief of the U.S. Children's Bureau, Edith chose to make her contribution to society as an educator, scholar, and analyst of public policy. Since it was highly unlikely at that time for an academic department like sociology or economics to hire a woman, Abbott first taught in the home economics program at the University of Chicago. The chance to teach in social work, and then to head the new School of Social Service Administration, provided Abbott with a life-long career. It also fueled her determination to help create a new profession—social work—where women could play a major role (Leighninger, 1987; Popple & Leighninger, 1999).

"Education for Social Work" covers a wealth of topics relevant to social work education both in 1915 and in the year 2000: the best way to structure field work, the role of the professional school in selecting people appropriate for a social work career (what is sometimes termed "gatekeeping" today), the relationship of a professional school to the university, and the difference between courses in the social sciences and courses in social work. She even broaches the topic of whether social work should be taught at all on the the undergraduate level, anticipating a debate between educators in undergraduate programs and those in graduate schools which will emerge in force some 25 years later.

Zilpha Smith's paper on field work gives further detail on the state of "laboratory training" for social workers, as it existed in 1915 at the Boston School for Social Workers, where she served as Associate Director. Already the important elements of field work are in place: the "guide" (today's supervisor), the "associate" acting for the school (or Field Director), a system of consultation between agencies and the school, and the format of a general placement in the first year, a more specialized one in the second. One difference, perhaps worth exploring today, is the use of two different agencies in the second year placement, to give the student an experience with two different specialties.

Finally, this monograph ends with selections from social work's first text book, Mary Richmond's *Social Diagnosis*, published in 1917. Richmond's book remained a classic text for many years. Helen Harris Perlman, whose own book, *Social Casework: A Problem-Solving Process* (1957) held a similar position in social work education, found *Social Diagnosis* on her desk when she began work as a social worker in the 1930s (Perlman, 1983).

One reviewer of Richmond's book called it "the only comprehensive textbook on social work in relation to the individual or family ever written," and stated, "It will be fully appreciated by the keen-minded, honest-purposed social workers who have eagerly awaited its advent, and whose highest hopes have been justified. It is a great book by a great teacher" (Sears, 1917, pp. 261–262).

Another reviewer, the sociologist Robert E. Park, noted:

> *Social Diagnosis* is, in short, the first notable attempt to formulate the practices and fund the experience gathered by social workers during a quarter-century of clinical practice and experiment. During this time welfare work, or social work,... has become an occupation and a profession....With this book social welfare work has ceased to be a mere body of traditional practices and is in a way to become a science....Social work thus becomes, not merely beneficent, but intelligible. (Park, 1917, p. 952)

In her 1897 address calling for formal training in social work, Richmond had spoken of the need to move toward "certain established principles as underlying all effective service." Now, a number of years later, she was attending to that task. In her work of uncovering and conceptualizing these common principles, Richmond anticipated the activities of the Milford Conference, which in 1928 affirmed the existence of a "generic casework" with fundamental principles and methodologies cutting across all of casework's various specialities (Leighninger, 1987, pp. 12–13). In fact, in depicting the common skills and approaches within a broad profession, Richmond's approach can be seen as a forerunner of today's generalist social work.

Richmond's text thus contributed greatly to the content of social work education. Reading it today, one is struck not only by its efforts at conceptualizing and synthesizing, but also by the timelessness of much of the material. Richmond speaks, for example, of the "sympathetic study of the individual in his social environment," a concept of person-in-environment still basic to social work practice. Her sections on "outside sources," while quaint, are not all that different from discussions by today's social workers of their use of "collateral" information on clients. Her section on the new technology of the telephone reminds us of the confidentiality issues related to our new technologies of computerized records and the Internet. Her descriptions of the "First Interview" give a good picture of the struggle of this new field to impose some structure on what had been a fairly haphazard approach to understanding human problems. Overall, Richmond gives us a snapshot in time of social work's early attempts to regularize its practice and create an effective, communicable way of working with people in their environment.

༄༅

Edith Abbott

Hull House, Chicago

Education for Social Work*

The most recently organized professional schools are those that prepare for what is somewhat vaguely called "social work." No attempt will be made here to enter upon a discussion of the vexed question of whether or not "social work" is a profession.[1] The schools of philanthropy are organized on the assumption that social work is a profession for which the necessary training can best be given in a specially organized school of professional character....

An account of recent progress in the training of social workers means in effect an account of the history of the professional training schools for social workers in this country, since the oldest of these schools has a history of little more than a decade. This is not because social work, or social service, has been recently developed. Social work is new only in its professional aspects. Agencies, public and private, for the service of the destitute go back many hundred years in the history of England, and in this country they are as old as the colonies that were planted by Englishmen on the New England coast. But in the last decade of the nineteenth century the great increase in the number of permanent salaried positions in social work for properly qualified young men and women has given to such service a professional character that was lacking in the old days of more or less casual volunteer work. With the multiplication of agencies to serve the dependent groups in the community, the destitute, unemployed, sick, aged, the various groups mentally and physically defective, and with the increase in the number of organizations designed to promote social and civic reforms there has come a pressing demand for persons properly equipped to carry on this work....

---

* From Department of the Interior, U.S. Bureau of Education, *Report of the Commissioner of Education for the year ended June 30, 1915*, pp. 345–359. Washington, DC: Government Printing Office.

[1] A most important discussion of this subject will be found in the forthcoming report of the Baltimore sessions of the National Conference of Charities and Correction. The report will include papers by Mr. Porter Lee, of the New York School of Philanthropy, chairman of the conference committee on education for social work, and by Mr. Abraham Flexner, of New York, and Prof. Felix Frankfurter, of the Harvard Law School.

Before the organization of the professional school the social worker was either trained through the system of apprenticeship alone or he learned from his own mistakes. Thus the training of social workers resembled the early methods of education in the older professions of law and medicine. Like social workers, "doctors," we are told, "have after a fashion been made by experience, i.e., their patients paid the price." Mr. Abraham Flexner shudders at the cost of early medical education, for, he says: "The early patients of the rapidly made doctors must have played an unduly large part in their training." In much the same way the poor upon whom the social workers learned "what not to do" often paid heavy costs in suffering or demoralization.

Eleven years have passed since the first professional school of philanthropy completed its first full year of training. These years have been marked by growth in many ways. There are now five of these schools, three of which offer two years of work....*

These years of growth have been marked also by great improvements in the organization of the courses within the schools. In the beginning the lectures were given by persons engaged in practical social work; today the five schools all have staff lecturers giving all their time and thought to the work of teaching and to the problems of school organization. In this respect again, the lines of development have resembled those of the older professional schools of law and medicine in which the teachers were in the beginning successful practicing lawyers and doctors. In the newer, as in the older professional school, the organization of a real faculty group has been one of the great steps forward....

Notable progress has been made, too, in the past decade in the organization of the curriculum of the professional schools of philanthropy. Since the purpose of all these schools is identical, viz, to provide instruction and training for those who wish to enter the profession of social work, the curriculum is much the same in all the schools. It consists in general of lecture courses and class work, inspection visits to social institutions in or near the various cities in which the schools are located, and most important of all, fieldwork or practice work with some social agency. The lecture courses and classes of the schools differ from the courses in applied sociology offered in many of the universities in that the courses in the professional schools deal with practice rather than with theory; they are courses in social treatment rather than courses describing social conditions. Students who have had, in

---

* *Author's Note:* Abbott goes on to describe the formation of "schools for social workers" in New York City, Chicago, Boston, St. Louis, and Philadelphia

the college or university, courses dealing with the causes of poverty or with social politics or similar subjects may have learned why social work is being done. The courses in the school of philanthropy endeavor to teach how it is done or how it ought to be done....

The most characteristic feature of the school curriculum, the feature that has most sharply differentiated the work of the school of philanthropy from that of the department of sociology in the university, has been the organization of field work, and upon this a growing emphasis has been laid. Field work in this sense has come to mean a system of social apprenticeship. From the first, the professional schools have realized that social work could not be undertaken without actual practice work in the office of a good social agency; that students could learn how to do only by doing under expert supervision. Comparison may be made between the field work of the school of philanthropy and the clinical experience furnished by the good medical school. Certainly the stress laid upon clinical practice for the medical student resembles the emphasis upon field work in the training of the social worker....

In attempting to explain more concretely what has come to be known as field work in the curriculum of the professional school, it must be understood that as the term "social work" is used to describe widely varying activities, so the term "field work" has come to describe widely different kinds of practice work. The most important of these is the apprenticeship with case-work agencies, since the technique of case treatment is fundamentally necessary for almost every social worker; but other kinds of field work that are essential as training for more specialized work are (1) work with some governmental or quasi governmental agency, such as an efficiency bureau or a bureau of sanitary inspection, for those who wish to enter more specifically civic work; (2) participation in the recreational work of settlements or other neighborhood centers; (3) investigational work for those who wish the necessary technical training in methods of social inquiry.

Mr. Flexner's account of the interrelation between the medical school and the good clinic serves to illustrate the ideals which the schools of philanthropy and the social agencies of their respective cities have in mind in arranging "field work" for students. The student in these medical clinics, in the words of Mr. Flexner, "gets by assignment a succession of cases, for a full report upon each of which he is responsible; he must take the history, conduct the physical examination, do the microscopical and other clinical laboratory work, propound a diagnosis, suggest the treatment." That is:

> The student is a physician practicing the technique, which, it is to be hoped, may become his fixed professional habit; learning through experience, as indeed he will continue to learn long after he has

left school—a controlled, systematized, criticized experience, however, not the blundering helpless "experience" upon which the student hitherto relied for a slow and costly initiation into the art of medicine....

If the importance of "field work" in the curriculum is accepted, there would seem to be a definite limit to the number of schools that can be properly organized, a limit that would be determined by the number of cities in which good field work could be found. Professional training schools for social work should be established only in cities where good social work is done. The establishment of such schools will in all probability be confined, of necessity, to a few large cities, and will probably make impossible the development of such schools in connection with universities or colleges situated in the country or in small towns. As a way out of this difficulty, it has been proposed to have the student proceed to a term of nonresident work which is to be devoted to field work in some city after the classroom work has been completed in the university—a plan of more doubtful value, since the importance of correlation between field work and class work is regarded as essential, if the student is to derive proper training from either....

No attempt will be made in this report to discuss the progress that has been made in universities and colleges in increasing the number of courses in applied sociology. It may be noted that in general such courses are not professional in character....In general the schools of philanthropy are professional schools of graduate rank.[2] The percentage of

---

[2] The catalogue of the Chicago School of Civics and Philanthropy for the year 1914-15 contains a somewhat detailed statement of the status of the school in relation to the work done in the universities:

The Chicago School of Civics and Philanthropy is not identified with any university. Representatives of several university faculties are trustees of the school. The work done is often recognized by various universities and credit given on application; the standard maintained is, however, rather that of the professional than of the graduate department, and the methods attempted are those applied in courses of law and medicine rather than in the theoretical and general work in economics and sociology. These methods, as has been shown, involve the combined use of the lecture upon methods of work, the classroom discussion of special problems, and practical work under the direction of efficient social agencies.

Our social [job] exchange, however, is frequently embarrassed by applications for positions in social work from students who believe they have had training for such work through graduate courses in economics

THE SHAPE OF EMERGING PROFESSIONAL EDUCATION   59

students who already hold college or university degrees has steadily risen in all the schools, until in some of them approximately two-thirds of the students belong in this group. The courses in applied sociology developed by the universities are designed almost exclusively for undergraduates, and the question must be faced, both by the schools and the universities, as to whether training of the kind developed in the schools is suitable for undergraduate students. For many kinds of social work a degree of maturity greater than that possessed by the vast majority of recent college graduates is requisite. With regard to the relationship between the professional schools and the graduate schools of the university, it may be pointed out that there are difficulties, grave but perhaps not insuperable, in the way of adjusting the curriculum of the professional school to the requirements, for example, for a master of arts degree. The question of credit for field work in its present somewhat unstandardized condition is perhaps the greatest difficulty. At present, it may be said, the schools of philanthropy are rendering a unique service. They are not duplicating university courses in their classrooms, and in their attempt to organize and standardize the practice work that is called "field work" they are engaged in experimental work which can best be carried on outside of the more rigid and formal requirements demanded by a system of university credits for university degrees....

In conclusion, a brief summary may be made of the most important indications of progress in education for social work within the past decade. The number of professional training schools for such work in the United States has increased from three to five; all the schools have improved greatly in material equipment; some of them now have excellent libraries, and two of the schools are housed in buildings exclusively devoted to school purposes; one of the schools is already pro-

---

and sociology. Such students may have had courses or seminars which deal with the causes of poverty, the labor movement, phases of modern industry, or theories of social reform. They have not had, however, any experience either in the field or in the office. They may have learned why social work is being done; they have not learned how to do it; and it is therefore impossible to recommend them for positions which require the skilled and delicate treatment of difficult situations when their fitness for such work has never been tested. Obviously, the distinction should be carefully drawn by the college student who anticipates entering the field of social service between graduate study leading to the advanced degree on the one hand and the professional school of philanthropy with its carefully arranged system of social apprenticeship on the other.

vided with a large endowment, and the budgets of the other schools have become more adequate to their needs. More important signs of progress are the improvements in school organization and administration, the increase in the number of permanent staff lecturers, the solidifying of the curriculum, the gradual standardization of the requirements for field work. Largely as a result of the improved facilities of the school, there has been a great increase in the number of students and a still greater improvement in the "grade" of student as evidenced by the rising standards of entrance requirements in most if not all of the schools. A further indication of progress is to be found in the contributions that have been made by the schools to the literature of social work and social investigation....

As to that hoped-for result of the training schools for social work forecast so long ago by Miss Richmond in her paper at the Toronto conference (the progressive reaction of the improved professional standards of the schools upon the work of social service), it is as yet too early to speak. It is, however, obvious that, as a result not only of the training given in the schools, but through the process of selection that is exercised through the agency of the schools,[3] the selection of new workers who have met the tests provided during the year's period of training, there will be a gradual improvement in the character and quality of social work. Any improvement, however gradual in the body of social workers, must in the long run improve the character of social work. Speaking at the last National Conference of Charities, Mr. Porter R. Lee, whose rare experience combines that of superintendent of a large charity organization society and of staff lecturer in the New York School of Philanthropy, presented an admirable statement of this fact:

> It may not be amiss to point out that it rests largely with social workers themselves whether their calling shall rise to the plane of a profession or sink to the level of a trade....The collection and interpretation of facts in a large body of knowledge is the foundation of any profession....Social work will still grow from an occupation to a profession just as rapidly as its practitioners develop this

---

[3] See the report of the committee on "Securing and Training Social Workers," presented at the Boston meeting of the National Conference of Charities, in which Miss Breckinridge, of Chicago, as chairman of the committee, made the following statement: "There is, too, reasonable unanimity as to one function which these schools may serve—that of selection. The conscious elimination of the incompetent and the unfit is a task of no mean importance when the object of our service may so easily become the victim of our blunders."

body of knowledge out of their experience and acquire the power to apply it. When this committee [on education for social work] considers on the one hand how easily social workers assume the mantle of expertness, and on the other how long and how painstaking is the process by which the older professions have come to authoritative leadership, they could wish for social workers of this generation, as part of their endowment, nothing more earnestly than the spirit of humility in the face of their unparalleled opportunity.

Zilpha D. Smith

Associate Director, Boston School for Social Workers

Field Work*

The essential necessity of field work and class work combined in the training of a social worker has been so adequately expressed by Miss Abbott, that I go on at once to speak of certain principles which seem to underlie getting from field work its full educational value, and of their application in Boston where the surrounding conditions differ somewhat from Chicago.

First, as to these conditions.

A social worker in Boston, as in Chicago, would like a student volunteer to give to that one agency many hours a week—but none of those to whom we send students has suggested that the work done in an average of seven hours a week has not both disciplinary and educational value. Before the schools were organized there had been growing up in settlements, in the associated charities and elsewhere, the practice of training volunteers who offered only a few hours a week—of leading each on from one task to another more difficult or more responsible.

And now graduates of the school take part in this field work training, a half-dozen as head-workers, many more as assistants under whom the students work, and a considerable group as members of boards. These more than others appreciate the student's peculiar difficulties and opportunities—but many not graduates, including some who come from social work in other cities, show equal faith in organized training, and give willingly, even eagerly, cooperation in that training. Should the number of students exceed the number of possible assignments offering training of quality, the schools will surely find it much wiser to reduce the number of students by careful investigations of applicants ... than to use training places that are undesirable. It is fair to both the learner and the trainer to send no one to even the most efficient social worker during the first six months in a new position and never to send to an agency more students than it is quite willing to take.

The wish for more time for practice-work is one with which I sympathize so strongly that I should like to linger on the plan of our second year which gives weeks and months of practice in some one sec-

---

* From *Proceedings of the National Conference of Charities and Corrections*, pp. 622–626. Chicago: Hildmann Printing Company, 1915.

tion of social work, in an educational progression which is not practicable for a single agency to arrange fully; and fortifies this with other experience and with specialized and advanced class work; the aim being to make the worker both skillful and flexible—able to do the same kind of task well even in new and surprisingly different situations, equipped with practical working knowledge of the various ways of administering an agency and of organizing the charitable spirit and the public spirit of the community to give it support and volunteer service. That is, the second year aims to send out a worker already fitted to undertake an independent or semi-independent position.

But both such a well rounded, yet specialized, second year for the few—and the slower single-line training of paid work for the many—need an earlier year of school work in which the questions as to practice-work are not so simple. The aim of the first year is to give a broad understanding of social work in its various phases, and to send out workers much less skilled than from the second year, but able to cooperate with all other social workers in understanding and sympathy. The schedule has been again and again studied and revised, and no more than one-third can be spared for practice—only fourteen hours a week.

The plans for using these fourteen hours are determined by several considerations:

First. The student is at the threshold of social work and needs to test himself—more often herself—and his chances of finding that particular kind of social work to which he will be most glad to contribute, are increased by trying himself in two kinds.

Second. Contact with his guides and with other workers is important for the student's education, and also for his future, because their judgements of him open or close the way to further training or to employment. These judgements often differ, and if both guides observe the student through the whole year—a year so rich in new knowledge and experience that the student often shows at the end a very different reaction from that near the beginning, or even at mid-year—the judgements of his guides are more discriminating and just.

Third. An even more important educational reason for working with two agencies from the beginning to the end of the year, is the opportunity thus gained to carry in each a relationship with two families, or with several children placed out, or with a few persons on probation, or with a club or class in a neighborhood house—steadily through the whole eight months. This gives the student opportunity to show initiative; to get at first hand "the long view"; to see things happen, perhaps to make them happen. New powers unfold under this responsibility long-continued.

So important are these three considerations—testing the student in two kinds of social work, securing judgements that are discriminating and just, carrying long responsibility—that, although often some one of the guides suggests a change to fourteen hours a week in one agency at a time, *no group* of guides after talking the matter out has ever recommended such a change.

Attendance is expected at such meetings of conference, committee or staff, as may help the student to relate his own special task to the whole work of the agency, and to understand its form of organization....

We cannot make a highly skilled worker in fourteen hours a week in eight months, but we can give a practical understanding of what technique means, show how much there is still to learn, and help a student to discover his aptitudes and to choose, or be chosen in the field of work in which these aptitudes may best be cultivated and used.

For most students, we prefer that the two agencies be associated charities and neighborhood work. The associated charities, through its weekly conferences, makes the student acquainted with a number of volunteers and with representatives of various specialties in social work (and makes them acquainted with the student), and also gives experience in problems where the family is the center. The settlement includes study of a neighborhood as a neighborhood rather than as the setting for a particular family, and uses the group method....

The two preferred agencies, the associated charities and a neighborhood house, give acquaintance with different districts, chosen because they are different and will help the student to appreciate the neighborhood background and to cooperate with its various elements, even if work later undertaken be for children or patients widely scattered. However, we use other agencies, as more than half our students come already desiring to specialize. A few have already specialized and feel the need of a broader or a longer view. We try to discover both the wish and the need of each student, and to meet both. We send students to child-placing societies, to medical social service, to a probation officer, and occasionally to other kinds of work.

Written reports from both student and guide, interviews and telephone conversations are frequent, and suggestions for rounding out each student's development from anyone of the four persons concerned—the student, her two guides in the field, and the associate acting for the school, are helpful to the other three. An outline of the class program for the current month is sent to each field-work guide, and some of them take pains to turn into the student's hands practical work which will bear on the current class subjects. On the other hand, the order in which subject follows subject in our class work has been modified somewhat for its effect on the student's practice.

The school owes one duty to the agencies which has not yet been mentioned—the duty of bringing together now and then the workers in each kind of field-work who guide students, and with them when practicable members of their committees or boards, to exchange ideas and experiences as to the training of our students, and of any other volunteers....

The guides say these conferences to which we invite them help their work, and they surely help the school to interpret the field work. Miss Abbott has spoken of the need of class exercises for this; there is often need of individual interpretation also, the worker having given the student a good educational succession of minor tasks and failed to make the student understand what their educational significance is, or which of the student's powers they have tested or disclosed. The conferences of workers help the associate at the school to interpret the worker's plans to the individual student, each according to need.

Mary E. Richmond
Social Diagnosis*

Preface

Fifteen years ago, I began to take note, gather illustrations, and even draft a few chapters for a book on Social Work in Families. In it I hoped to pass on to the younger people coming into the charity organization field an explanation of the methods that their seniors had found useful. It soon became apparent, however, that no methods or aims were peculiarly and solely adapted to the treatment of the families that found their way to a charity organization society; that, in essentials, the methods and aims of social case work were or should be the same in every type of service, whether the subject was a homeless paralytic, the neglected boy of drunken parents, or the widowed mother of small children. Some procedures, of course, were peculiar to one group of cases and some to another, according to the special social disability under treatment. But the things that most needed to be said about case work were the things that were common to all. The division of social work into departments and specialities was both a convenience and a necessity; fundamental resemblances remained, however.

With other practitioners—with physicians and lawyers, for example—there was always a basis of knowledge held in common. If a neurologist had occasion to confer with a surgeon, each could assume in the other a mastery of the elements of a whole group of basic sciences and of the formulated and transmitted experience of his own guild besides. But what common knowledge could social workers assume in like case? This was my query of fifteen years ago. It seemed to me then, and it is still my opinion, that the elements of social diagnosis, if formulated, should constitute a part of the ground which all social case workers could occupy in common, and that it should become possible in time to take for granted, in every social practitioner, a knowledge and mastery of those elements, and of the modifications in them which each decade of practice would surely bring.

This narrowed my proposed topic to the beginning processes of case work, but at the same time widened it enormously in demanding for its treatment an experience of all the various types of such work. As the executive head, in those days, of a large family agency, I had little

---

* From *Social Diagnosis*. New York: Russell Sage Foundation, 1917; reprint New York: Free Press, 1944. Reprinted here with permission.

time for study so the task was set aside for nearly nine years.

More than six years ago, however, after I had become a member of the staff of the Russell Sage Foundation, it was again taken up.

Meanwhile, the wider usefulness of social evidence, social diagnosis, and social treatment, both in their own special field and in the other professions, even when these latter dealt with people who were neither dependent nor delinquent, had begun to dawn upon me. It was evident that social case work could supplement the work of justice, of healing, and of teaching. Groups of workers in some of our American cities, moreover, were doing notable things in the regular social agencies; they were developing quietly a diagnostic skill in dealing with the difficulties of human beings which should be given ample opportunity, especially in its formative period, to grow to the full stature of social technique.

I turned to this task in the winter of 1910–11 for the second time, therefore, with a quite different outlook from that of earlier days and with the determination to push my inquiries as far beyond the limits of my own personal experience as possible.... [Richmond then describes a painstaking process of gathering information from many sources, including the records of case workers in a variety of fields, to study the ways in which workers gathered information about their clients.]

Chapter I

Beginnings

Though the social worker has won a degree of recognition as being engaged in an occupation useful to the community, he is handicapped by the fact that his public is not alive to the difference between going through the motions of doing things and actually getting them done. "Doing good" was the old phrase for social service. It begged the question, as do also the newer terms, "social service" and "social work"—unless society is really served. We should welcome, therefore, the evident desire of social workers to abandon claims to respect based upon good intentions alone; we should meet halfway their earnest endeavors to subject the processes of their task to critical analysis; and should encourage them to measure their work by the best standards supplied by experience—standards which, imperfect now, are being advanced to a point where they can be called professional.

The social workers of the United States form a large occupational group. A majority of them are engaged in case work—in work, that is, which has for its immediate aim the betterment of individuals or families, one by one, as distinguished from their betterment in the mass. Mass betterment and individual betterment are interdependent, however, social reform and social case work of necessity progressing together. This fundamental truth will appear repeatedly as the present discussion of social diagnosis advances.

Since social case work is too large a subject to be covered in one volume, its initial process alone will be the subject of this book.

When a human being, whatever his economic status, develops some marked form of social difficulty and social need, what do we have to know about him and about his difficulty (or more often difficulties) before we can arrive at a way of meeting his need? The problem may be one of childhood or old age, of sickness, of exploitation, or of wasted opportunity, but in so far as it concerns some one individual in his social relationships it is not alien to social work as here understood. The effort to get the essential facts bearing upon a man's social difficulties has commonly been called "an investigation," but the term here adopted as a substitute—social diagnosis—has the advantage that from the first step it fixes the mind of the case worker upon the end in view. The primary purpose of the writer, in attempting an examination of the initial process of social case work, is to make some advance toward a professional standard....

[In 1897,] Edward T. Devine, secretary of the New York society, made a strong plea for improvement in the personnel of the investigators, for their training, and for a clearer definition of the end which investigation has in view. In the following year he organized the summer course of training which was to develop later into the New York School of Philanthropy, the first of the training schools for social workers established in this country. The opening of these schools gave a strong impetus to developments already under way in social agencies. It became more apparent than ever, for example, that investigation was not merely a notion of the charity organization societies, that this process was essential wherever the reinstatement of a human being was to be attempted. On the other hand, practical instruction in social diagnosis and treatment was made possible for the school students by the case work opportunities (analogous to the "bedside opportunities" in medical instruction) offered to them from the beginning by the charity organization societies and later by other agencies. Case work cannot be mastered from books or from class room instruction alone, though both have their place in its mastery....

Chapter VI

The First Interview

We turn now to the details of social case work method. It will be necessary to remember that in any art the description of its processes is necessarily far more clumsy than are the processes themselves. In the last analysis moreover, the practitioner of an art must discover the heart of the whole matter for himself—it is of the essence of art that he shall win his way to this personal revelation; but an intimate knowledge of the successes and failures, the experiences and points of view of his fellow practitioners will be found to be essential too. The thirteen chapters that follow attempt to analyze the experiences of case workers in their daily use of the four processes which lead to social diagnosis.

These four processes are (1) the first full interview with a client, (2) the early contacts with his immediate family, (3) the search for further insight and for sources of needed co-operation outside his immediate family, (4) the careful weighing in their relation to one another of the separate items of evidence thus gathered and their interpretation. By interpretation is meant the attempt to derive from all the evidence as exact a definition as possible of the client's social difficulties—the act of interpretation is the act of diagnosis.

It cannot be assumed that any one of these processes is always completed before another begins. When the First Interview is held in the client's home, contacts with the family often overlap our first contact with the client. As soon as we have two statements instead of one, whether these come from the family or from outside sources, we begin to reason about them, to compare them, and to draw certain tentative inferences from them. Nevertheless there are these four processes, distinguishable despite their interplay.

Many social workers are of the opinion that the most difficult and important is the first—the initial interview. Probably this is the part of the diagnostician's task in which personality, as contrasted with technique, counts for the most, for here he should establish some basis of mutual understanding and get some clues to the evidence which will shape his judgment later. "I am more and more convinced," wrote the secretary of a large family agency years ago in a personal letter, " that the finished skill of a good social worker is most shown in this first visit or interview. No knowledge of general principles, no cleverness in gaining cooperation, no virtues in the worker, and no committee, however wise, can make up for want of skill in gaining quickly the confidence of the family, and getting the foundation for all good work to follow."...

The Place of the Interview. The place in which the First Interview is held depends in part upon the nature of the task and its origin, but not wholly upon these. Societies dealing with questions of family relief and, in these later days, with family rebuilding have changed their policy several times with regard to the place of the interview. Following the line of least resistance, the older type of worker usually conducted

First Interviews at this office desk, with record form before him and pen in hand. He asked each question in the order indicated by the items on the form, and filled in a short summary of the perfunctory reply before going onto the next: Assistance asked? "Coal and groceries." Cause of need? "Out of work." Any relatives able to assist? "No."

As a reaction against this stupid compiling of misleading items, many American case workers have abandoned the office interview.... It is their practice to take only time enough, when application is made at the office, to assure themselves that treatment is probably needed, and then promptly to make a visit to the home, where, in an unhurried talk, the basis is laid for further acquaintance.

The arguments in favor of holding the First Interview in the home instead of in the office are, in family work, (a) Its challenge to the case worker at the outset to establish a human relation, at the risk, if he fail, of coming away without the simplest and most elementary data. In the office, clients are on the defensive and justify their visits by their replies. In the home, the social worker is on the defensive; the host and hostess are at their ease. (b) Its avoidance of the need of so many questions, some of which are answered unasked by the communicative hostess and by her surroundings. To the quiet observer the photographs on the wall, the framed certificates of membership in fraternal orders, the pensioner's war relics, the Sunday school books, the household arrangements are all eloquent. And far more revealing than these material items are the apparent relations of the members of the household to one another—the whole atmosphere of the home. (c) Its provision of natural openings for a frank exchange of experiences. "The great facts of birth and death alone are sufficient to make the whole world kin," and these and the universally interesting comparison of diseases form a good basis for that kind of informal intercourse which belongs to the fireside. Then, if some of the children are present for a part of the time at least, there is a good chance for comparing notes about brothers and sisters, their ages, names, namesakes, etc....

Here, then, we have the attitude: a cheerful willingness to listen to the present symptoms which seem so important to the one interviewed, but a quiet determination to get below this to a broader basis of knowledge, by carrying the client's mind forward to hopes and possibilities ahead, and backward to the happier, more normal relations of the past. And since, if we would help him, we must break through the narrow circle of our client's own view and get into the wider one of those who know and understand him, we must depend upon the First Interview for those clues which are most likely to supplement and round out his story. "I never mean to leave a family," says a case worker of long experience, "until I have some clue or other for obtaining outside information, no matter how long it takes me to get it."

It would appear, then, that the objects of a First Interview are fourfold:

1. To give the client a fair and patient hearing.
2. To establish, if possible, a sympathetic mutual understanding—a good basis, that is, for further intercourse.
3. To secure clues to whatever other sources of information will give a deeper insight into the difficulties of his situation and their possible solutions.
4. To begin even at this early stage the slow process of developing self-help and self-reliance, though only by the tonic influence which an understanding spirit always exerts, and with the realization that later the client's own level of endeavor will have to be sought, found, and respected....

A number of case workers have been asked to write as careful an analysis as possible of the process of some of their own recently held First Interviews....

These analyses were not needed to prove, though they do prove, that the worker must at once begin, as soon as the interview opens, to draw certain tentative conclusions—they are little better than conjectures at this stage—and must also be prepared to abandon these as the interview and the later story develop. Take, for instance, one of the analyses at hand in which a man, out of work for several months, applies to a family agency in a city to which he had just come with his wife and child. In answer to the first comment of the interviewer that she understands he is a locomotive engineer, he volunteers the statement that he was disqualified by "nervous trouble" in November and has not worked since. At once there comes to mind some outline of the things that the vague phrase "nervous trouble" might cover. Is the disease physical? Mental? A result of some habit, of alcoholism or drug-taking? The very first line of questioning takes the direction of finding out what kind of medical care the man has had. This brings the name and address of a doctor in another town, whose advice can be sought later. But the possibilities further suggested by "nervous trouble"—such as drug habits, etc.—lead the worker somewhat later to cover carefully the man's whereabouts since his discharge, his means of maintaining his family, his reasons for leaving his farmer father with whom he and his family have been staying, etc. At any moment, either during the interview or later, information obtained may show that some one or more of the hypotheses that prompted the questions asked are untenable. They must never be clung to obstinately....

These processes of reasoning, of inference, of making a first hypothesis as a tentative starting point, have been considered in Part 1, and following the gathering of evidence, its correlation, as discussed much later, involves a reweighing of inferences already drawn; but any interview in which the social worker was not using his reasoning faculties in this way every moment would be lifeless and useless....

There is no one way of conducting a First Interview, and it may be that upon occasion any one of the foregoing methods might have to be resorted to, but the more flexible method of the worker who keeps his mind open to all natural avenues of approach and utilizes them to the full is likely to yield better results in the long run and in the majority of cases....

Bringing the Interview to a Close. The test of a successful interview, we should remember, is twofold. We must have succeeded in getting enough of the client's story and of the clues to other insights to build our treatment solidly upon fact; and we must have achieved this, if possible, without damage to our future relations, and with a good beginning made in the direction of mutual understanding. Interviews that have covered every item of past history and present situation with accuracy and care can be total failures. Interviews that have led to an enthusiastic acceptance on the part of the client of the social worker's point of view, and a lively anticipation of much benefit from future intercourse, can also be failures, though failure of the second kind need not be so fatal and complete as that of the first. We are not investigating for the sake of investigating, but for the sake of getting something done that will be permanently helpful.

In our effort to build a solid foundation we may have had to ask some embarrassing questions and touch a nerve that is sore. It is most important, where this has been the case, that in the last five or ten minutes of the interview we dwell upon hopeful and cheerful things, and leave in the mind of the client an impression not only of friendly interest but of a new and energizing force, a clear mind and a willing hand at his service....

Emergency Interviews. There are cases of severe illness or other emergency in which action is too urgently necessary or the conditions are too unfavorable to admit of more than a hasty First Interview. [One of these is described below]:

You cannot stop to find out whether the young Slav lying ill with typhoid in the filthy lodging house came over in the North German Lloyd or the Red Star Line, or whether he embarked from Trieste or Hamburg. Uncle Sam must get along without this particular bit of information,...but while you are making things happen, do not forget your clues. You must know if Peter Novak has any relatives here or whether he belongs to any church or fraternal order. And once poor

Peter is provided for today, in a hospital if he will go or at home if he will not—he is too ill to be argued with—and you have these clues for the work that ought to be done on the case tomorrow, you will be justified in going on to your next interview.

Another story illustrates this matter of clues....The police had telephoned a case of destitution. Police cases are always said to be destitute, but as soon as the street and number were given the district worker knew that she should find some sickening form of human suffering. The house was a rear tenement containing three apartments of two rooms each. One of the three she knew as a disreputable resort; in another three children had been ill with diphtheria the summer before; and in the third two consumptives had lived and died in succession. In these rooms she found a young man, scarcely more than a boy, in the last stages of consumption. He was in a sullen state of despair and weakness and would not talk. He had no people, he said—a brother somewhere but he did not know where he was. He had no friends and no one to care about him. He had made his bed and would lie in it.

Just here nine charity workers out of ten, perhaps, would have hurried away, after seeing that food was provided for the present need, to send a doctor and the district nurse, and to order milk and eggs to be sent to the poor fellow every day until he died. This particular charity worker did nothing of the kind. It was growing late and she had several other visits to make, but how could she leave this poor fellow with no knowledge of him but his terrible present? Even in the midst of filth and the ravages of disease she could discern that somewhere in the past which he refused to disclose he had known the comforts of a good home. This was a case for slow persistence and searching question; the social surgeon must not falter. At last the name of a former employer slipped out. The young man learned his trade there. Good! That former employer carried on a well known business and would know the youth without doubt. Forty-eight hours after that interview, the sick boy was under his father's roof. His parents were respectable, well-to-do people, who had tried to bring up their son in the right way. He had fallen into bad company and evil ways, and two years before had left home in a violent passion after some of his wrong-doing had been discovered. Lately, his people had heard a vague rumor that he was ill and had telephoned to the different hospitals in the city, but had given him up for lost. When last seen by his interviewer, he had been given the best room in his father's house, a room with the sun in it all day; his people were giving him all the milk and eggs that he needed and would be glad to have the nurse call. Surely it was worth while to take time for such a result....

Chapter VIII

Outside Sources in General

Reasons for turning not only to a client's family group for insight and advice but to Outside Sources have been suggested earlier. The chief reason for seeking this further help is that, to be constructively useful, we must be able to break through the narrow circle of the client's own view of his situation, and the narrow circle also of our own prepossessions and favorite modes of procedure. We cannot afford to adopt either of these circumscribed boundaries, because none of us lives on a desert island.

Can our client's affairs ever be regarded as ready for social treatment when no Outside Sources have been consulted? Measuring by the standard of concrete result instead of preconceived theory the answer would be in the affirmative. Cases studied for this book show correct diagnoses that were arrived at without any follow-up visits to outside references, but they also show a great preponderance of failures traceable directly to this omission.

Essential almost always is personal communication with some of those shown by the records or by the client's story to have known him at an earlier time and in quite different ways. Our relations with these Outside Sources collectively and separately will be considered in this [chapter]....

Statistics of Outside Sources

1. A Study of the Sources Most in Use. Social workers have been so busy doing their work that they have had little time in which to formulate its processes or its results. There have been no data available as to sources of information, for instance, either as to those sources that were consulted at all, or as to the particular combinations of sources that had been found most valuable in each different form of social work. The processes in which social agencies are actually engaged, the things that they are doing, are often quite different from what they think they are doing. Accordingly, a first, very imperfect attempt has been made to get this matter of Outside Sources upon a basis of fact by asking a variety of social organizations to permit the study of 50 case records in each....Public and private relief departments, public and private child-placing and child-caring agencies, societies to protect children from cruelty, day nurseries, home and school visiting activities, juvenile and adult probation work, charity organization societies, and medical-social service departments were among those included in this small piece of research. Information from certain of these social activities would, in some places, have had to be very fragmentary, because often scant records are kept or none at all; but three American cities were chosen, representing three different stages of development in social work for individuals, and, in so far as the condition of their social agency records would permit, the forms of work already indicated were covered in each city. It was possible to examine the records of 19 different types of social organization. [See Table 2]....

Other things being equal, the social worker who, in addition to the sources that are almost universally valuable, consults the most diverse sources of information for diverse tasks and diverse cases, is doing the best work....

Chapter IX

Relatives as Sources

What does the reading of case records and the evidence of case workers, in so far as it has been possible to collect this in many interviews with them, show as to Relatives? Clients often do not want their Relatives seen. Why is this, and what mistakes of the social worker may justify, at least in part, this position? More and more social workers are seeking out Relatives, though more and more they are discovering their bias, and the need of sifting their evidence with great care. Just what is gained in accuracy of diagnosis and effectiveness of treatment through this source which can be had in no other way? From the data at hand, what is the case for and the case against Relatives as helps in social service, and more especially in its initial stages?...

II. The Case for Relatives

Experience throws into bold relief the prejudice and the un-wisdom of Relatives, but there is plenty of evidence on the other side which shows that in actual daily practice social workers are not only securing (1) individual and family history from kinsfolk, but are finding them a fountainhead of (2) insight (a more important matter than history), and also an effective source of (3) backing and active co-operation.

1. Individual and Family History. "Too often," writes a case worker, "we consider simply the individual family and say, 'This man drinks,' 'This woman is not a good housekeeper,' when as a matter of fact a study of the family background would give us an insight into causes. This background comes best from the relatives."...

Relatives, then, are our main reliance for family history, for the story of those traits and tendencies, those resemblances and differ-

Table 2. — Order of Frequency of Consultation in the Separate Cities of the 20 Sources[a] Most Often Used in the Three Cities Taken Together[b]

Order of Frequency of Use in the Three Cities	Source	Order of Frequency of Consultation in the		
		First City	Second City	Third City
1	Relatives	1	1	4
2	Present neighbors	9	3	1
3	Physicians	2	9	3
4	Friends	6	6	2
5	Former employers	5	7	6
6	Hospitals and sanatoria	4	8	10
7	Teachers and principals	7	2	17[g]
8	Clergymen	8	11	8
9	Present landlords	18	4	5
10	Present employers	10	10	9
11	Former landlords	16	5	16
12	Police	3	17	18[g]
13	Dispensaries	14	14	12
14	Former neighbors	13	12[d]	15
15	Courts	17	13[d]	14
16	Nurses	19	21[e]	19[g]
17	Health departments	20	16	28[h]
18	Lawyers	21[c]	25[f]	22
19	Present tradesmen	29	24	20[i]
20	Fellow church members	22[c]	39	13

[a] Exclusive of private and public charitable and social agencies.

[b] The 20 sources most used in the three cities taken together were selected as follows: For each city all the sources were numbered in order of frequency of consultation, beginning with the source most frequently consulted. The numbers indicating the order of frequency of each source in the three cities were then added together. The 20 sources showing the smallest resulting totals are included in the table.

[c] Same number of consultations with lawyers and fellow church members, in records of first city.

[d] Same number of consultations with former neighbors and courts, in records of second city.

[e] Truant officers were consulted same number of times as nurses, in records of second city.

[f] Lodgers were consulted same number of times as lawyers, in records of second city.

[g] Same number of consultations with teachers, with police, and with nurses, in records of third city.

[h] Former tradesmen and foreign consuls were consulted same number of times as health departments, in records of third city.

[i] District or county attorneys were consulted same number of times as present tradesmen, in records of third city.

ences in a family stock which we are learning to regard as of far-reaching importance....

2. *Insight.* Some items of evidence have social significance because they suggest new sources of information or possible helps in treatment later on, while others are valuable because they help us, at a time when we have felt balked and unable to decide how to proceed, to grasp at once the core of the difficulty. Relatives are not the only sources that can give these sudden insights, but they so often point the way in what have been no-thoroughfare situations, that case workers have become almost superstitious about the one Relative who has not been seen.

Even when the Relatives are unco-operative their stories are revealing. "I remember one instance," writes a worker, "where the mother flatly refused to aid the daughter's family in any way, where the brothers and sister were too self-absorbed to share with their sister even in her great distress. Yet the stand these people took, in all its ugliness, pictured the story vividly—a disobedient, ungrateful daughter and selfish and careless sister, a woman who would, in all probability, make an indifferent wife and mother. This knowledge was a service in planning the method of attack in that particular family."...

A case record that came to the attention of the writer last year covers more than a hundred pages in reporting successively the work of four different districts of one charity organization society with the Braucher family, the man an American in his late thirties with a South American wife and two small children... In transferring the treatment of this family from the third district to the fourth, the secretary making the transfer wrote that it had been impossible to verify most of the family's statements, that Braucher had failed to follow instructions when good medical care had been procured for him, and that the family "showed industry as beggars but in no other way."

About fifty pages of the record are filled with accounts of futile attempts to get some basis of fact on which to operate, followed by attempts to befriend the family and to improve, on the very inadequate data at hand, their physical and economic condition. The man's people lived in another city, but the local charities there had given nothing more definite, in reply to inquiries, than the statement that the Relatives had been known to them and that they had "a discouraging record."

The secretary of the fourth district, taking advantage of a trip to the neighborhood of the man's early home, visited the charities formerly interested in his Relatives, read the "discouraging record," found that her client's mother was still living (he had reported her as dead, and seems to have believed that she was), looked up her address with the aid of directories, had a long talk with her and gave her the first news of her son in many years. He ran away from home when he was only sixteen, and his father, it appeared, had deserted the family before that. This personal visit to another city gave the charity organization society its first real insight into the background of its client. The mother revealed strong family feeling and she and her immediate family showed a certain degree of resourcefulness.

The secretary returned with a cordial message from her and an offer to entertain one of the little grandchildren, whose very existence had been unknown to the Relatives before. Armed with this invitation and with news of the man's people, a fresh appeal was made to him; his plans and purposes were reviewed in a long friendly talk, and, from that time, it was evident that an interest which appealed to him, a plan of life which touched his imagination, had a last been presented. His first ambition was to make a good appearance when he visited his mother, as he did soon after. His wife also began to share with him the ambition to have a better home, to which his mother could be invited on a return visit. At last there seemed to Braucher to be a good and sufficient reason for taking the few steps necessary to make medical treatment, so ineffective before, truly effective.

In less than a year's time after the discovery of these Relatives, the charity organization society was able, with the aid of the family affection and the new social interest brought into their lives, to transform these difficult clients into people who carried responsibility more cheerfully and were more interested in their little home. The steps by which this was achieved are apparent enough in the matter-of-fact pages of the record, which show that no magic was employed, and that the measure of success achieved was no accident, based, as it was, upon the insights and the interests which a group of Relatives in no sense remarkable—they had once been described as "difficult"—had been able to supply....

Chapter XVII

Letters, Telephone Messages, etc.

...As a means of communication within the city, especially with other social agencies, the telephone is very popular among case workers and will probably continue to be so. Its dangers and shortcomings are only beginning to be noted, and they deserve enumeration for this reason. No one will use the telephone too little because it is so convenient, but the facts brought to light in the course of our case reading should lead everyone to use it, in diagnosis, with more caution.

It is comparatively easy to get in communication with even a very busy person over the telephone, which still has the right of way in household and office alike. But this very fact means that the one telephoned to may have been interrupted, with the result that he is somewhat irritated and has little conscience about putting off the interrupter with an inadequate and hastily expressed statement. Are the ordinary run of people as frank in their telephone intercourse as they are in intercourse face to face? The question is not without interest. When an attempt is made to answer it, this factor of interruption will have to be taken into account. Another consideration will have to be the fact that the one telephoned to cannot always be sure of the identity of the person at the other end of the wire. How can he know that this questioner is just what he claims to be? The one telephoning, on the other hand, cannot know who is in the same room with his informant, and the informant cannot always be sure, unless he has a private wire, who else, besides the people in the room with him and the questioner, may be listening to the conservation.

Two other elements increase the chances, not of suppression or untruthfulness, but of error. Over the telephone, as we now know it, proper names are very frequently and other words somewhat less frequently misunderstood. In case work this is a serious drawback. In addition to this, case records seem to show that the eye helps the ear in noting what is said, and that telephone conversations are less accurately reported on our records than are personal interviews. The following comments and case items illustrate these drawbacks:...

> The husband of a tuberculous wife asked a medical-social department to communicate with him by telephone, when necessary, at the factory where he worked. But in this way the fact that his wife had tuberculosis became know there, and the fear among his fellow employees that he might infect them made it so uncomfortable for him that he was forced to leave....
>
> A family agency was asked by a society in another city to see the relatives of one of its clients and his physician. The agency telephoned to the physician to find that the client's brother was in his office at the time. While the treatment of the case was not hampered by this fact, it made an additional difficulty for the brother, who was extremely sensitive about the client's misfortunes.
>
> A child-protective agency operating in a rural area reports that, in the small country towns included in its district, half the town may be on one telephone line, and that is it considered an innocent and legitimate diversion to lift the receiver and hear all about one's neighbors. This is especially true if a particular neighbor is known to have had a visit from the agency's case worker....

Chapter XVIII

Comparison and Interpretation

II. The Comparison of Material

"I am astonished," says Dubois, "to see how many young physicians possessing all the working machinery of diagnosis do not know how to make a diagnosis. It is because the art of diagnosis does not consist merely in gathering together a great many facts, but in coordinating those that one has been able to collect, in order to reach a clear conception of the situation."[1]..."After a student has learned to open his eyes and see," writes Dr. Richard Cabot of clinical teaching, "he must learn to shut them and think."[2] So must we. Nevertheless, this stage of assembling our material, of relating its parts and trying to bring it up into consciousness as a whole, will not be easy to illustrate, since it is the most neglected part of case work technique.

The social case worker of an earlier day did little visiting of anyone except his client and so observed only within those narrow limits. He was mentally sluggish, moreover, and guilty of much thoughtless prescribing. The case worker of today is more active physically—sometimes doing too much running around, one is tempted to believe—but his advance in usefulness over earlier workers would be greater if he would oftener "shut his eyes and think," if he would reduce the visible signs of his activity and assemble his forces in order the better to deliberate upon his next move before he makes it. Case records often show a well made investigation and a plan formulated and carried out, but with no discoverable connection between them. Instead, at the right moment, of shutting his eyes and thinking, the worker seems to have shut his eyes and jumped. On the other hand, however carefully the inquiries are recorded and the diagnosis which grew out of them indicated, however carefully a plan of action is decided upon, etc., the processes by which the diagnosis is arrived at—what parts of the evidence have been accepted or rejected and why, what inferences have been drawn from these accepted items and how they have been tested—can none of them be revealed in a record.

Some case workers feel that their conscious assembling of material comes when they present a summary to the case committees of volunteers who assist them in making the diagnosis and the plan of treatment....

---

[1] The Psychic Treatment of Nervous Disorders, p. 277.
[2] Case Teaching in Medicine, Introduction, p. vii.

The same bracing influence comes from submitting findings at this stage to a case supervisor who is responsible for the work of a group of social case workers. Indeed, the process of comparison, in so far as it can be studied at all at present, is found at its best in the daily work of a few experienced supervisors. Unfortunately they are usually persons who are much overburdened....Either supervisors or committees have the advantage over the worker who makes his analysis unaided, that they do not know the client or his story, and that consequently they are not already so impressed with any one part of the story as to be unable to grasp the client's history as a whole....

III. The Interpretation of Material

Ability to form a judgment is more important than ability to suspend judgment. We are between the horns of a dilemma here, for the diagnosis too promptly made, even when not erroneous, may be only the one-word diagnosis which roughly describes the general type of difficulty, and leaves undefined every individualizing particular. The delayed diagnosis, on the other hand, may miss the critical moment for effectiveness in treatment. With all the defects apparent in the social handling of the Ames case, [a case discussed earlier in the text] it shows ability to grasp promptly the significant factor in a human relation—in this instance, the wife's unwillingness to have her husband leave home, and the reason for it. It is this insight into human relations that distinguishes social diagnosis from all other kinds....

Sometimes where there has been frequent change of social agency or of worker in a case, every type of diagnostic habit will be found in a single record—the one-word diagnosis, the situation-of-the-moment diagnosis, the painstaking but fumbling kind, the clear-on-the-main-difficulty type, as well as the type which is both clear and full.

Take, for example, the family of Braucher, the man with a South American wife and two small children, whose story is told in part in the chapter on Relatives. The family, it will be remembered, had been treated in four different districts of one charity organization society. First, the situation was summarized as "man unable to work because of flat-foot; distress of family due to this case." Later, when Braucher had neglected the medical treatment offered, and when routine efforts to verify his story had failed, it was summed up in the phrase, "family shows industry as beggars, but in no other way." A local charity in another city had offered, as a definition of the characteristics of the man's relatives, who lived there, the statement that they were people with "a discouraging record." But the secretary in the fourth district, dissatisfied with this report, had sought out Braucher's people and brought back to him a message from them. The message appealed to an unsuspected side of the man's nature—a fact which this fourth social diagnostician, unprejudiced by earlier verdicts, was prompt to recognize. The renewal of Braucher's relations with long estranged kindred became the worker's starting point in the attempt to develop his social and industrial ambitions, these ambitions becoming in turn the keynote in a long and successful treatment. With all this, Mrs. Braucher's separate needs were not overlooked. Social diagnosis should not limit itself to the naming of one cause or one disability.

It would be possible to maintain, of course, that the worker who succeeded where three had failed had a stronger faith in human nature or a more winning personality. Unquestionably these were factors in the success. As has been said elsewhere, faith in the possibilities of our clients and of social treatment is fundamental. But the turning point was the discovery of the relatives by one who knew how to weigh evidence and to follow slight clues. Success was due to technique and insight in combination.

1. Diagnosis Redefined. Social diagnosis, then, may be described as the attempt to make as exact a definition as possible of the situation and personality of a human being in some social need—of his situation and personality, that is, in relation to the other human beings upon whom he in any way depends or who depend upon him, and in relation also to the social institutions of his community....

Chapter XIX

The Underlying Philosophy

Although mention has been made more than once in earlier chapters of the interdependence of individual and mass betterment, it will not be amiss, in bringing this long discussion of the diagnostic process to a close, to re-enforce briefly the position already taken that social reform and social case work must of necessity progress together. We have seen, for example, that the diagnostic side of case work received a great impetus when the plans of reformers began to be realized, and that social work immediately had at its command more varied resources than it could apply without further knowledge of the differences between men. To understand these differences and adapt its working programs to them, account has had to be taken of men's social relationships.

Less emphasis is placed in these pages upon the other side, upon the number of social reforms that have been direct outgrowths of case work, and the number that owe to this work either effective amendment or successful administration. There are few administrative tasks in the social field, in fact, which do not have to utilize some form of social diagnosis and treatment. A new piece of social legislation may give case work a new direction, it almost always modifies such work, and sometimes renders it unnecessary in a given field. This last eventuality, however, is predicted many times for once that it is realized.

When, for example, the restriction of child labor was made possible, several new kinds of case work became necessary, one of them involving greater skill in sifting the various evidences of age, one involving the development of other family plans to take the place of children's earnings, etc. The methods of many agencies engaged in case work were modified by these child labor measures. In some states, on the other hand, data supplied by the agencies pointed the way for improvement in the new laws. Discussing this subject of the relation of case work to social reform at a recent session of the National Conference of Charities and Correction,[1] the writer ventured the opinion that workmen's compensation laws belonged to the type of social legislation which rendered further case work for one group unnecessary. But in the debate which followed several people were on their feet at one time to bring forward instances in which case workers had not only had to make adaptations of the existing compensation laws to individual cases, but, in so doing, had discovered points at which these laws should be amended....

The important fact for us is that, while readjustments are clearly necessary, diagnosis and therapy do assuredly assume, with each advance in social reform, each gain of scientific medicine, not less but more importance in both fields. If, as we have seen, the one-word diagnosis of our case work cannot be social, neither can the single reform put forward to cure all the ills of society. There is, in fact, more resemblance than either would admit between the mental habits of the case worker who contentedly treats one individual after another, one family after another, without giving a thought to the civic and industrial conditions that hedge them about, and the mental habits of the reformer who is sure that the adoption of his particular reform will render all social case work unnecessary. Both ignore the complexity, the great diversity, of the materials with which they are attempting to deal....

It will still be necessary to do different things for and with different people, and to study their difference, if the results of our doing are to be more good than bad. It will still be necessary to study the social relations of people, not only in order to understand their differences

---

[1] See *Proceeding of the National Conference of Charities and Correction* for 1915 (Baltimore), p. 43.

but in order to find a remedy for the ill that will continue to beset them. These ills will change their form, some will be blotted out, and the whole level of life, as we have a right to hope, will be lifted. Although the level upon which the case worker operates will also be raised, case work will still be needed; its adaptation of general principles to specific instances will not be automatic nor will good administration become so. It may also be predicted that the forms of organization now responsible for case work will change, that its scope and skill will advance far beyond the present-day practice described in this study. The methods and processes here dwelt upon will subordinate themselves to a large whole. It is only through devotion to that whole—not through any narrow insistence upon technique alone—that we can submit ourselves in the right spirit to the task of analyzing individual situations.

References

Austin, D. (1997). The institutional development of social work education: The first 100 years—and beyond. *Journal of Social Work Education, 33*, 599–612.

Brackett, J. (1903). *Supervision and education in charity.* New York: Macmillan.

Brackett, J. (1906). Training of social workers: Report of the committee. In A. Johnson (Ed.), *Proceedings of the National Conference of Charities and Correction* (pp. 445–451). Columbus, OH: F.J. Heer.

Carlton-LaNey, I. (Ed.). (1994). The legacy of African American leadership in social welfare [Special issue]. *Journal of Sociology and Social Welfare, 21*(1).

Coohey, C. (1999). Notes on the origins of social work education [Letter to the editor]. *Social Service Review, 73*, 418–421.

Costin, L. (1983). *Two sisters for social justice: A biography of Grace and Edith Abbott.* Urbana: University of Illinois Press.

Dore, M. M. (1999). The retail method of social work: The role of the New York School in the development of clinical practice. *Social Service Review, 73*(2), 168–190.

Ehrenreich, J. H. (1985). *The altruistic imagination: A history of social work and social policy in the United States.* Ithaca, NY: Cornell University Press.

Flexner, A. (1910). *Medical education in the United States and Canada.* Bulletin no. 4. New York: Carnegie Foundation for the Advancement of Teaching.

Johnson, P. (1978). Black charity in Progressive era Chicago. *Social Service Review, 52*, 400–415.

Karpf, M. J. (1925). The relation of schools of social work to social agencies. In *Proceedings of the National Conference of Social Work.* (pp. 650–658). Chicago: University of Chicago Press.

Leighninger, L. (1987). *Social work: Search for identity.* Westport, CT: Greenwood.

Lennon, T. (1999). *Statistics on social work education in the United States: 1998.* Alexandria, VA: Council on Social Work Education.

Lubove, R. (1969). *The professional altruist: The emergence of social work as a career, 1880-1930.* New York: Atheneum.

Park, R. E. (1917). Review, Social diagnosis [Review of the book]. *Journal of Political Economy, 25*(9), 952–954.

Peebles-Wilkins, W. (1995a). Frazier, Edward Franklin (1894–1962). In R. L. Edwards (Ed.-in-Chief), *Encyclopedia of social work* (19th ed., p. 2586). Washington, DC: NASW Press.

Peebles-Wilkins, W. (1995b). Washington, Forrester Blanchard (1887–1963). In R. L. Edwards (Ed.-in-Chief), *Encyclopedia of social work* (19th ed., p. 2616). Washington, DC: NASW Press.

Perlman, H. H. (1983, October). Interview with author, University of Chicago.

Pittman-Munke, P. (1986, March). *Sisterhood is powerful: The role of women's clubs in the early career of Mary Richmond.* Paper presented at the Social Welfare History Symposium, Annual Program Meeting of the Council on Social Work Education.

Popple, P., & Leighninger, L. (1999). *Social work, social welfare in American society* (4th ed.). Boston: Allyn and Bacon.

Pumphrey, M. (1986). Mary Ellen Richmond. In W. I. Trattner (Ed.), *Biographical dictionary of social welfare in America* (pp. 622–625). Westport, CT: Greenwood.

Ross, E. L. (Ed.). (1978). *Black heritage in social welfare, 1860–1930.* Metuchen, NJ: Scarecrow Press.

Scott, A. F. (1993). *Natural allies: Women's associations in American history.* Urbana, IL: University of Chicago Press.

Sears, A. (1917). Social diagnosis [Review of the book]. *American Journal of Sociology, 23*(2), 261–262.

Shoemaker, L. M. (1998). Early Conflicts in Social Work Education. *Social Service Review, 72*(2), 182–191.

Specht, H., & Courtney, M. (1994). *Unfaithful angels: How social work has abandoned Its mission.* New York: Free Press.

Starr, P. (1982). *The social transformation of American medicine.* New York: Basic Books.

Taylor, G. (1905). Report of the Committee on Training for Social Workers. In A. Johnson (Ed.), *Proceedings of the National Conference of Charities and Correction* (pp. 436–444). Columbus, OH: F.J. Heer.

Trattner, W. (1999). *From poor law to welfare state: A history of social welfare in America.* New York: Free Press.